Basic
Auto Repairs

BY BYRON G. WELS

GROSSET
GOOD LIFE
BOOKS

PUBLISHERS • GROSSET & DUNLAP • NEW YORK
A FILMWAYS COMPANY

Acknowledgments

Cover photograph by Mort Engel
Drawings by Scott Swink

The author wishes to express his appreciation
to the following for permission to use their
illustrations: AC Spark Plug Division of
General Motors: p. 6, p. 51, p. 52, p. 53, p. 54,
p. 55, p. 56, p. 57, p. 58, p. 59, p. 60; and tables
p. 61, p. 62, p. 63, p. 64; Hand Tools Institute
(from *Striking and Struck Tools* © 1973 and
Wrenches and Pliers © 1974 by Hand Tools
Institute): p. 11 bottom; p. 12, p. 13 bottom,
p. 35, p. 83; Stanley Tools, division of The
Stanley Works: p. 13 top, p. 23; Xcelite, a
member of The Cooper Group: p. 11 top.

For Joan, Vicky and Caroline

Contents

1
Fix Your Own Car— Can You? Should You?

The reasons for thinking positively when it comes to fixing your own car are myriad. Costs are escalating. The services of your local mechanic are sky-rocketing in cost, and this is not the fault of the mechanic, either. His own costs are constantly rising, and to stay in business, he must pass those costs on to you. It also becomes increasingly important that you keep your car in top operating condition, for a small problem can quickly become a large and expensive one. Most of the small problems are easy for you to correct yourself, *while they're still small.* And by doing them then, you avoid the need for costly repairs later on. There's another important factor too: by making small adjustments, you can cause your automobile to operate more efficiently. The car that operates efficiently will cause less air pollution, will be more economical in its use of fuel, and you can't find any fault with saving fuel!

Economy-Wise

Here's an example of the kind of savings we're talking about: every time you apply the brakes, you cause the brake-lining to press against the brake drum located in the wheel. Naturally, abrasion takes place, and the brake lining wears a little bit. On some cars, the brake lining is held in place on the brake shoe by rivets. These rivets are normally sunk below the surface of the lining, but, should the lining wear sufficiently, they can become exposed. When they are, the rivets rub against the brake drum and you hear the characteristic squeal of metal-on-metal. What you do not hear, but can well imagine, is the groove that the rivet is making in the drum.

To correct this situation, the drum must be ground down to its original smooth condition. If you do not have the drums ground, the score-marks created by the rivets will only cause the new brake linings that you will install to wear away more rapidly than they need to.

By changing the brake linings before the rivets are exposed, a relatively simple job, you can save yourself the need for dismounting the wheels and paying your local mechanic to grind the drums. In addition, since grinding the drums reduces metal in it, in time the drum will become so thin that grinding will no longer be feasible. A new brake drum will then have to be installed and more money invested. All for want of new brake linings.

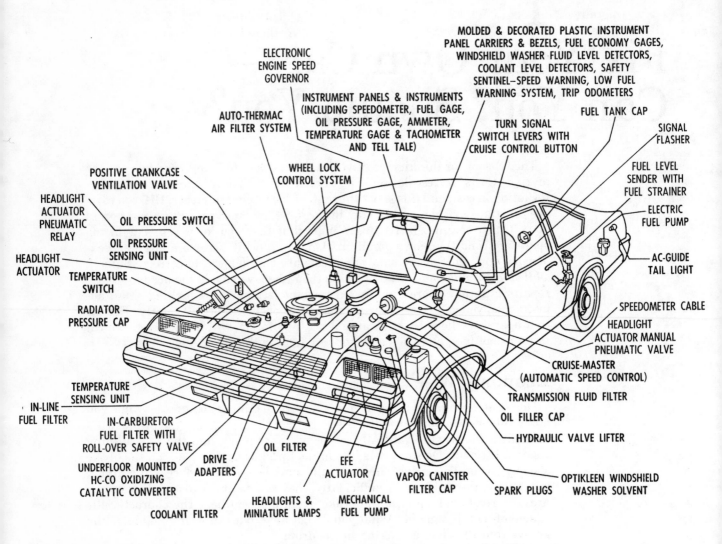

ELECTRONIC
ENGINE SPEED
GOVERNOR

MOLDED & DECORATED PLASTIC INSTRUMENT
PANEL CARRIERS & BEZELS, FUEL ECONOMY GAGES,
WINDSHIELD WASHER FLUID LEVEL DETECTORS,
COOLANT LEVEL DETECTORS, SAFETY
SENTINEL—SPEED WARNING, LOW FUEL
WARNING SYSTEM, TRIP ODOMETERS

FUEL TANK CAP

AUTO-THERMAC
AIR FILTER SYSTEM

INSTRUMENT PANELS & INSTRUMENTS
(INCLUDING SPEEDOMETER, FUEL GAGE,
OIL PRESSURE GAGE, AMMETER,
TEMPERATURE GAGE & TACHOMETER
AND TELL TALE)

TURN SIGNAL
SWITCH LEVERS WITH
CRUISE CONTROL BUTTON

SIGNAL
FLASHER

POSITIVE CRANKCASE
VENTILATION VALVE

WHEEL LOCK
CONTROL SYSTEM

FUEL LEVEL
SENDER WITH
FUEL STRAINER

HEADLIGHT
ACTUATOR
PNEUMATIC
RELAY

OIL PRESSURE SWITCH

ELECTRIC
FUEL PUMP

HEADLIGHT
ACTUATOR

OIL PRESSURE
SENSING UNIT

AC-GUIDE
TAIL LIGHT

TEMPERATURE
SWITCH

SPEEDOMETER CABLE

RADIATOR
PRESSURE CAP

HEADLIGHT
ACTUATOR MANUAL
PNEUMATIC VALVE

CRUISE-MASTER
(AUTOMATIC SPEED CONTROL)

TEMPERATURE
SENSING UNIT

TRANSMISSION FLUID FILTER

IN-LINE
FUEL FILTER

OIL FILLER CAP

IN-CARBURETOR
FUEL FILTER WITH
ROLL-OVER SAFETY VALVE

HYDRAULIC VALVE LIFTER

DRIVE
ADAPTERS

UNDERFLOOR MOUNTED
HC-CO OXIDIZING
CATALYTIC CONVERTER

OIL FILTER

EFE
ACTUATOR

VAPOR CANISTER
FILTER CAP

OPTIKLEEN WINDSHIELD
WASHER SOLVENT

SPARK PLUGS

COOLANT FILTER

HEADLIGHTS &
MINIATURE LAMPS

MECHANICAL
FUEL PUMP

It helps to learn the correct names for auto parts—and use them.

Can You Do It?

There are a lot of jobs in and around the car that you should be willing to do for yourself. You probably empty the ash trays, add oil or water when it's required, wash the car, and even peek into the battery cells to see the water level is where it should be.

But there are other jobs that people tend to avoid. While they are right in avoiding some of these tasks, there are others that they could perform with relative ease, if they only knew how. And that's what this book is all about. We're going to show you how to tackle some of those previously "hands-off" jobs, show you how to save a lot of expense by doing it yourself, and, at the same time, you're going to learn how doing these jobs correctly—when they need doing—will help prolong the useful life of your car.

Unfortunately, in the case of auto repair, success can sometimes breed failure. Too many people, flushed with early success, will attempt to go too far in working on their cars. We do not want you to do that. Some jobs simply must be relegated to a competent mechanic who possesses the skills and tools and experience to do those jobs properly.

How to Use This Book

To begin with, sit down and read the book quietly from cover to cover. Then you'll know exactly what and what not to expect from it. Go back and re-read portions that were not clear to you and, finally, read those sections again that apply to work you'd like to attempt yourself on your own car. When you feel confident that you are able to do the work described, then that's the time to begin.

It's very important, before you attempt any actual work, to know exactly and precisely what you are going to do and how you are going to do it. Automobiles differ from one another. While the principles are essentially the same, they do vary from car to car, from year to year, and from model to model.

Obviously, it is beyond the scope of a book such as this to delineate the specifics for each make, model, and year. You will have to apply the information here to the specifics of your own car. When we discuss the "positive crankcase ventilation" valve, for example, we are not going to tell you that it's in the upper-right side of the breather, or the lower-left of the engine block. We will simply explain that the valve is attached to the hose which runs from somewhere on the air breather to somewhere on the valve cover. As there is only one such hose, you will have no difficulty in locating it on your own automobile's engine. Having found this hose, it's a simple matter to pull the hose loose, examine both ends of it, and find the small valve.

Let's Make Cents

Another good reason for doing your own repairs: a mechanic working at a service station gets paid for two jobs. First, he must restore your automobile to proper operating condition, in other words: labor. Second, he is also paid for any replacement parts that he installs. The garage—his company—makes a good profit on replacement parts so, obviously, the mechanic is not about to repair those parts that can be repaired if he can make additional money by installing new parts! Take the spark plugs, for example. The job of a spark plug is to create a spark in the cylinder which causes the mixed and compressed gases to ignite and burn rapidly, so that the expanding gases will drive the piston downward. (This causes the crank shaft, to which the piston is attached, to rotate and the rotating power is transmitted to the drive shaft and the wheels.)

The spark plug consists of two metal elements supported in a ceramic-insulated collar. The elements are spaced a preset and given distance apart. In use, the metal elements tend to foul and become dirty, to burn and build up carbon deposits. When this happens, the plug functions improperly, the gases don't ignite, and you find that your car lacks response and loses fuel as well. The usual corrective step, as performed by mechanics, is to remove the old spark plug, throw it away, and replace it with a new spark plug.

This is not a bad thing to do, since new spark plugs cost about one dollar each, and you only need one for each cylinder in your car. A six-cylinder car, therefore, will require six spark plugs.

In our father's day, however, when parts were scarce and money was tight, spark plugs weren't simply tossed away. No. The mechanic would remove the old plugs, bring them into the garage and sand-blast the deposits away. He would then inspect the elements, and if they seemed to have sufficient life, he would re-gap and replace them. New plugs were installed only when the elements had been sufficiently burned away to warrant such replacement. Try to find one of those old spark-plug cleaning machines today. And a spark-plug file for dressing the elements? You'll have to search long and hard to find one of those, too!

In these days of planned obsolescence, buying new spark plugs every so often is considered a normal operating expense. We think nothing of replacing spark plugs that could last several additional thousands of miles. Is that really important? Of course. It's not simply a matter of one spark plug for one dollar. If you have a six-cylinder car, you're talking about six dollars, just for the spark plugs. If it's an eight-cylinder car, the price goes up to eight dollars! Yet, a little work with a file and a gapping tool, a bit of work with a wire brush and some cleaning fluid, and you can save the eight dollars. You'll probably manage a few thousand extra miles out of those plugs, too.

Should You Do It?

This brings up another point. Maybe you're "all thumbs." Maybe you can't hammer a nail straight. Does that mean you should not attempt this work? Let's look at another example. Supposing a light bulb burns out in your kitchen. Do you call in an electrician to change it? Of course not. You buy a new bulb, unscrew the old one, and screw the new one in its place. You might even have to remove a diffuser or lamp shade in the process, too. But changing the tail-light lamp in your car is actually a less-complicated operation, once you gain access to the lamp. You'll usually find a chrome trim piece that's held in place by a couple of

screws. Remove the trim, lift the glass lens out of the way, and there's the bulb. Press it in, give it a half-twist, and it comes out in your hand. On the base, just under the glass envelope of the lamp, you'll find the bulb's number. Your local automotive service shop can provide you with a replacement lamp. Press it in, give it another half turn in the opposite direction, replace the lens and trim assembly, and you're all set. By the same token, there are many tasks like this that you can do for yourself, easily and safely, without risk to yourself or to your car.

Another example is the quite commonplace problem of locating and repairing leaks in windows, doors, or the trunk. While you can take such a problem to any able mechanic and he will, in time, repair it, you will find that by using this book, and armed with the proper cement and caulk, you can effect a suitable repair with little or no trouble, and save yourself much heartache and cost.

Naturally, the biggest saving is connected with wear-and-tear on your car. By doing the work yourself, you save the cost of labor and you are more inclined to attempt other jobs that you might have waited for a mechanic to do. Holding off on repairs causes a chain of events to take place. A bad part gets worse. As it worsens, it affects other components as well. Nothing ever really "wears in" or gets better with time. The problems become more complex, and the repair bill, which is always the "bottom line," increases. When you do your own repairs, you do them as they are needed, thereby breaking the chain of expense. You reduce the chance of suddenly being confronted with a large built-up expense, and extend the car's useful life.

In addition, if you properly perform periodic and preventive maintenance, your car will last well beyond its allotted life and provide you with a better return when you sell it. What's more, when you *do* decide to sell it, it will be because you want a new car, and not because your car has succumbed to mechanical failure that is too costly to repair.

Impossible? Not at all. You may note that there are many people who own and run "classic" cars that are older than many of us! These cars are kept in perfect condition and run the way they did when they were new. Why? Because they are maintained and tenderly cared for. They don't rattle, don't burn excessive amounts of oil, and are expected to continue to perform for many years to come. Our concept of planned obsolescence—having a car run only as long as the bank payments last—is nonsense. Detroit changes a body line or a paint stripe, and we are conditioned to clamor to the dealer's for the current year's model.

Consider, too, that fuel costs are rising. The basic cost of raw material is going up, taxes on fuel are escalating, and anybody that drives or owns a car will want to do whatever he can to get more miles from a gallon of gas, and thereby reduce driving costs. Other factors enter into this as well. Anti-pollution devices, installed on newer cars, are required by law. While these function to remove the unburned products of combustion from the exhaust gases and will help to clear the air, they do away with good gasoline mileage. But the anti-pollution device will be with us for some time to come. It should please you to note that by doing a proper tune-up, and by making sure that engine components are clean, you can increase your car's mileage, even to a point that negates the mileage-loss caused by the installation of the anti-pollution device! To sum-up, anything you can do to squeeze more miles out of each gallon of gasoline will be well worth your time.

It's All Here

What you read in this book will describe tasks that you can usually do easily and simply. Instead of paying a mechanic to do the job, you can do it yourself, and the financial savings will be paid for with your own labor, the dirt on your hands, and the satisfaction of knowing that you accomplished something worthwhile for yourself.

Finally, read the book through completely and make whatever tests are required to keep your car performing well. Don't wait until problems develop. Put together your own program of *preventive* maintenance, rather than a haphazard one of *corrective* maintenance, and you'll keep your car on the road longer and running smoother.

A word of caution, though: most of the procedures outlined are simple and easy to put into effect, however, you should proceed with care. If you have to call on someone to put your car back together after you've taken it apart, it will be some time before you'll be tempted to try doing it yourself again. Go easy. "Get your hands dirty" by trying some of the minor operations first; then, with a few successes behind you, you'll be better prepared to tackle the major jobs properly.

2
Tooling Up

There are certain essential tools you should already have. Tools that you would not dare to be without. You've probably got a jack and lug wrench in the trunk of your car right now. You need those if you get a flat tire. There are other tools that you will need and use regularly if you're going to work on your own car. Some tools will be used less often than others, and still other tools will be used only occasionally, for certain specific jobs. Don't invest a small fortune in tools just yet, however. Let's discuss them first.

You Get What You Pay For

In general, you'll find varying quality in tools, and you are urged to get the best you can and make your first expense your last. You can buy a steel screwdriver with a highly-polished blade, a colorful plastic handle, and get it for mere pennies. But in short order, the blade will get chewed up, the handle will fall off or crack, and off you go to buy a new screwdriver. It makes sense to buy the best you can afford, and have the tools for the rest of your life. Our grandparents knew about this. Many of us have hand-me-down tools that are still usable and serviceable. It wasn't just that Grandpa took good care of his tools (which he did—and would—considering the cost), but he bought top quality.

Select Wisely

Never try to make a tool do work it wasn't designed for. A screwdriver is not an all-purpose tool; that's why they are often sold in sets. If you have a large screw to turn, use a large screwdriver. You'll find the tool to be more comfortable in your hand, the work will go more easily, and the tool (and screw!) won't get butchered up.

If you come across a phillips-head screw, by all means get a phillips-head screwdriver! Don't think you can do just as well with a small-blade screwdriver of the slotted type.

Protect Tools

Another problem is caring for your tools. Your nice, shiny set of tools can quickly develop rust if they are not properly taken care of. Many of us keep our tools in a tool box in the car's trunk. That's all right, providing the tools are lubricated. A light coating of oil will protect your tools.

Make sheaths for sharp or toothed tools, such as files and saws, to protect both you and the stored implement. You can form such sheaths from cardboard and masking tape. Do your files get clogged up? Coarse files should be lubricated *before* using, so the metal waste will simply drop out when the file is tapped. Stubborn pieces of waste metal in the file, or smaller files, will respond to a "file card" which is a wood board fitted with short, stiff wires, like a bristle brush. Use this on your file, and it will be as good as new.

Maintain your tools in good order. A handle falls off? Replace it with some epoxy cement as soon as you get the chance. Don't wait until you need to use it. Tools getting dull? Have them honed. Beginning to see tell-tale signs of rust or pitting? Get busy with some emery cloth and don't forget to oil the tools before putting them away.

You can also obtain a small bag of silica gel, which is a desiccant that will keep the area inside your tool box dry.

Now let's talk more specifically about the tools we're going to need in order to properly maintain the car.

The Basics

Those tools that we will always have on hand are the jack and lug wrench, of course. We will also want a screw jack (if we do not already have one) for those jobs that require us to work under the car. Never raise the car with only a bumper jack and crawl under it. If the jack lets go, as they have been known to do, the car can "bottom" when it falls, and you can be seriously injured. The screw jack is a lot safer than the bumper jack for these jobs, and should be supplemented by a set of roll-on ramps. Safety is the prime consideration.

Well-made tools, such as these metrically sized hex nut drivers, usually come in a protective case which can be used for storage.

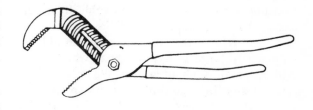

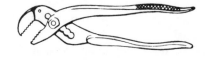

Both the slip-joint (top) and channel-lock (bottom) pliers can be locked into a wide assortment of jaw sizes for many types of jobs.

Get a good set of screwdrivers. The largest should be of a sufficient size to loosen the cylinder head bolts, and the smallest should be small enough to make those delicate adjustments on the carburetor. You will also want two phillips-head screwdrivers, in two sizes.

Pliers are also a necessary convenience, and we prefer the channel type that lock open and

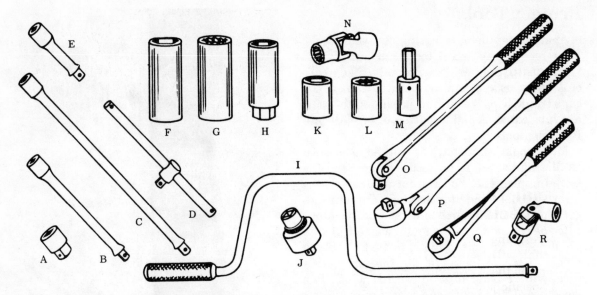

A set of hand socket wrenches might include: adapter (A), extension bars (B, C, E), sliding T handle (D), deep 6-point socket (F), deep 12-point socket (G), spark plug socket (H), speeder handle (I), ratchet adapter (J), regular 6-point socket (K), regular 12-point socket (L), hollow screw socket bit (M), universal 12-point socket (N), flex handle (O), flex head ratchet (P), reversible ratchet (Q), and universal joint (R).

provide sufficient strength for most jobs. You'll also want a good set of wrenches, and here, the best bet is the type with removable heads in assorted sizes, with proper handles, extensions, and a ratchet. The largest size should be sufficiently large to handle those wheel lugs, and the smallest about ¼ inch. We prefer offset wrenches of the type that are open on one end and closed, or "boxed" on the other. If you examine a wrench, you will see that the ends are slightly offset from the handles, so that by flopping the wrench end-over-end with each turn, you get a new "bite" and sufficient turning distance.

By the way, with the increasing use of metric sizes in the United States, in preparation for an ultimate changeover from the old style of measurement, if your car is of fairly recent vintage you may find yourself faced with a need for duplicate tools in the metrics. Don't hesitate to get these if you need them. You can be pretty confident they won't go out of style soon.

The open end or split box is perfect for tube fittings, but high torque situations call for a box wrench. This combination box- open-end wrench fills both uses.

We've also found good use for a ball pein hammer, and for a mallet with both a rubber and solid plastic face. You'd be amazed how handy this becomes when lug nuts stick on your tires.

Have a sharp knife handy, too. This is really the "universal" tool, for it can cut, scrape, remove insulation, trim, and do a number of tasks that make it well worth the small space it takes.

Keep an empty gasoline can in the car too. You *know* what this is for.

Have a handy electrical tester. Learn to use it. You'll also benefit greatly from a good-quality tire pressure gauge.

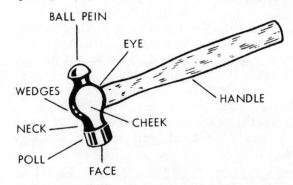

A few sharp blows on a well-placed chisel will loosen a rust-frozen screw.

And, if you'll be working under the car, we recommend a mechanic's sled. This is a wheeled platform with a comfortably-padded headrest that you lie on, and push to the desired position with your feet. You'll find that this handy tool is one of the most important aids you can get. The wheels are usually arranged so they "caster" or rotate in any direction. The sled can be purchased at any auto supply dealer.

Special Tools For Special Jobs

You're going to find use for certain other tools that will be employed only for specific jobs, and on those occasions when you are doing those specific jobs. Chances are that you can borrow such tools when they're needed, but if you prefer to have your own, by all means buy them—*you* will be using them.

For changing plugs and cleaning points, you'll need a spark-plug wrench, a gapping tool, and a small spark-plug file. A timing light will help you to check and set the car's timing, too.

We said you wouldn't require specialized tools, and here we are talking about a timing light that may set you back some fifteen dollars. The task of adjusting the car's timing is an important part of any professional tune-up. By doing this work yourself, you save substantially over the amount a mechanic would charge; and you can probably pay the cost of the light, then you have the light for the rest of your car's life.

You'll want a hydrometer for checking the specific gravity of your car's battery, and another (you can't use the same one) for testing the anti-freeze in your cooling system.

A torque wrench is another important tool that you'll use occasionally (and need when changing spark plugs) and you'll want a good-quality wrench for this job.

A brake adjusting tool is an inexpensive item that you will need to adjust your car's brakes. Due to its low cost, you'll surely want one in your tool kit.

As you set out to tackle those jobs on the car that require specialized tools, you can make

Designed for working in tight places, this new pocket-sized hack saw is still capable of cutting through a tailpipe to remove the muffler.

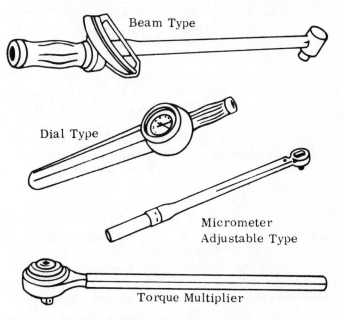

To tighten a fastener or part (such as a spark plug) to a specific number of pounds-per-inch pressure, use a torque wrench.

the decision then and there whether to borrow or purchase the tools. We recommend the purchase, where feasible, for once you have the tools, you will always use them.

Some Tools Not to Buy

Certain tools are used so infrequently that it hardly pays to buy them, or even mention them here. For example, you might want to sandblast your own spark plugs, but you'd have to sand a heck of a lot of plugs before this machine pays for itself. By the same token, a hydraulic tool for changing tires isn't worth buying unless you're in the business, for you'd have to change a lot of tires to make this device earn its keep—and the space required to store it.

If you're of a mind to take the dents out of your own fenders and then repaint your car, you can pick up a set of "dingers" and the other tools, supplement this with an air compressor and paint sprayer, and maybe—just maybe—you'll use these tools more than once! But don't go overboard, not just yet at any rate.

Take, for example, the sad tale of I'll-buy-it Jerry. He actually paid the rent at his local auto supply store, buying every new tool that came out. He was so well-equipped that he could do any job that came along. But Jerry soon found himself running a free tool-lending library, his neighbors and friends calling on him for those specialized tools (and advice) that they required. And, because he also knew cars, Jerry often found himself doing their work with his tools, usually for no more pay than a glass of beer when the job was finished. It just didn't pay.

So, unless you are planning to go into business, buy only what you need and don't want to borrow, as you need them. Furthermore, we don't recommend that you attempt to service cars for other people. This book is not designed to make you into an experienced mechanic overnight. Should you attempt to "help" a neighbor or friend, hard experience has shown that you will be held responsible for every subsequent failure in his automobile, whether the work you did has any bearing on that failure or not.

Accessories

The more involved you get with automotive work, the more you will wonder about the accessories that you will find offered. Chances are that you will be taken with one or more of these, and may decide to experiment.

One such accessory is a high-efficiency fan. You remove the standard four-blade fan from your car's engine, and install one of these multi-bladed, scientifically curved affairs that offers better and more efficient cooling. Chances are that if you've souped up your car to hot rod proportions and need that extra cooling, the high-efficiency fan will work wonders for you. If your car tends to overheat in the summer, it would again be worthwhile experimenting with.

Another thing you can add is a water-injection system. In this, a controlled amount of water is added to the fuel-air mixture that is fed to the carburetor. Now we used to inveigh against the idea, but we noticed that on rainy days our car performed a lot better. It was peppier. Noticeably so; appreciably so. We looked into the business of water injection a bit more deeply.

Water is incompressible. By occupying space in the compressed gas in the cylinder, you reduced the amount of space in the cylinder, pretty much the way you would if you shaved the cylinder head, a procedure used by hot rodders to boost engine performance. Again, how much you would benefit from this, or if you benefited at all, can be determined only by experimentation.

We should also note at this point, that the greatest inefficiency in an automobile is the man behind the wheel. Man drives pretty much out of habit, and may be inclined to do those things that reduce efficiency.

There's one accessory that comes in handy: a large-diameter gauge that fits atop the steering wheel column and has a three-color face. When the indicator is in the red, you're doing something wrong, such as jack-rabbit starting or lugging the engine. Keep the needle in the green, and you're driving with optimum efficiency. This small device can re-train your driving habits to provide longer engine life and extended gasoline mileage.

3
How and Where to Begin

There are two things that we don't want to see injured—the first, of course, is yourself. If you are careless, and do not follow instructions properly, there is the possibility that you might hurt yourself. We do *not* want this to happen. That's why we repeat again and again, know precisely what you are going to do and how you are going to go about it, *before* you do it!

The second thing we want to protect from injury is your automobile. Make certain that you follow each and every step in the sequence as outlined. When you do a disassembly procedure, the steps will be outlined for you. The parts will be identified. Remove them in the proper sequence and reassemble them in the proper sequence. When you clean a part, place the cleaned part on a clean, lint-free cloth or paper towelling. We want the reassembled component to be in better condition than it was before you took it apart. This will not be at all difficult if you take pains to follow the steps outlined.

Keep Things Neat

Since we don't want your spouse or family to look upon your efforts with a jaundiced eye, make it a rule never to bring greasy parts into the house for cleaning. The family bathtub may seem like an ideal place to clean and degrease, but if you leave it looking like the underside of the car, your efforts won't be very welcome in the future. It is easier, and better for family relations, to buy a large, plastic tub to use in the garage for such jobs. And, when you've finished your work, always end the job by carefully wiping your hands in the garage, then use a bit of special soap or detergent and water from the garden hose. Don't clean up in the bathroom, and leave a black residue for someone else to clean.

Your clothing is another important factor. It's a good idea to get a set of coveralls which will completely protect it. Even work clothing can be kept neat if you wear these. If you do not bother with suitable work clothes, we can guarantee that no matter how careful you are, your good clothes will *become* work clothes in the very near future.

Happily, things have changed a bit for hand care, too. There are a lot of adjustments you will want to make on your car that make the use of gloves impractical. With even the thinnest of rubber gloves, you will still miss the "feel" of your bare fingers, so don't plan on using gloves for hand protection.

In the old days, there was a product known as sand soap which was gritty and pasty. No matter how much grease you got on your hands, all you had to do was scoop up a few fingers full of this stuff out of the can, wash your hands and the grease vanished. (Except for any that found its way under the fingernails, the mark of an old-time mechanic.) Today there are similar soaps and detergents on the market, but one outstanding product that I'm sure you will like is a cream that is rubbed into the hands, before starting to work, and which dries on the skin. No matter how greasy your hands get while you work, when you're finished you simply flush the hands under water, and the grease and cream disappear down the drain.

A similar product is applied in the same way, but when you are finished with your work, you simply strip the dried material off each hand like a glove. The grease comes away, leaving the hands completely clean. Take care, though, how you use this, especially if you have hairy wrists.

Finally, before we get entirely off the subject of cosmetic cleanliness, a young lady friend taught us something else that we've found valuable. Before working on any messy, dirty job, dig your fingernails into a cake of soap, loading the under-nail area with the soap. This keeps the gook and dirt from getting under the nails and, of course, the soap washes away easily when the job is finished.

You'll want to keep the car itself clean, too. A good, careful service station attendant always spreads a drop cloth over the fender when he's leaning over it to work on the engine. This protects the fender paint from being scratched by his belt buckle and buttons, and surely, you must have heard the comment of the irritated lady who asked the garage attendant, "Where do you wipe your hands when you don't have a convenient steering wheel?"

Be extremely careful to leave the work area as clean as possible. A clean, organized job will always be a good job.

Of course, you can carry anything to extremes. One young do-it-yourselfer, after completely cleaning the engine block, painted the whole thing with white enamel. He then started the car and let it run until the block heated and the paint dried. "This way," he said, "I can see exactly where the oil leaks are taking place!" We certainly do not recommend this procedure.

But before you so much as take a screwdriver to the car, we suggest that you take the car to a local car wash that is equipped with a steam jenny. This unit generates live steam under high pressure—steam that will cut through the caked-on grease and grime around your engine. After the steam jenny treatment, the engine will be completely clean on all its outer surfaces. It's a good investment, and one that can be had at low cost.

Clean-up, too, is an important part of any reassembly procedure. If, for example, you are putting in a new carburetor kit, you will disassemble the carburetor, and will install several new parts on the old frame. The old parts that are to be thrown out can be ignored, but you should completely clean the old frame and housing which are to be re-used, before you start to reassemble the parts.

How do you clean such a unit? There are many degreasing chemicals that are designed to do this job. It's an easy matter to soak the component in the degreaser, remove it, hose it down, degrease it again, wash it thoroughly and towel it dry. It should then be allowed to air-dry thoroughly on a lint-free surface. But always follow such a cleaning immediately with a spray of light lubricating oil, for after degreasing, the part has no lubricant at all on its surfaces, and will practically rust before your very eyes. The lubricant you apply also assures that the parts will fit together more easily and will function properly.

Plan the Work

Working on an automobile is not something that you do arbitrarily or carelessly. It must be slow and methodical. You must know precisely what you are going to do and how you're going to do it, before you start. A great deal of discipline is a necessity. You always come across cartoons showing an idiot-type ripping his car's engine apart piece-by-piece, looking at each part without the least idea of what he's looking for, and then winding up with a pile of parts that he doesn't know what to do with. It's funny all right—but it's not that funny!

Planning is needed, too. You won't get far taking the old spark plugs out of your car and then getting in to drive down to the service shop for a set of replacements. Why? Because without the spark plugs the car won't start! Make sure that you've got everything that you need, and *then* set to work.

It's important to work in an orderly, problem-eliminating fashion, too. Instead of removing all the old plugs first, we're going to change one spark plug at a time. In that way, we eliminate the possibility of connecting the wrong wire to the wrong plug.

Know what you are going to do, get dressed for it, gather together the tools and equipment you will need—rather than risk being annoyed and the job held up by not being able to find the tool you need when you need it. Then set things up around the car in a place suitable to the work to be done.

You've got to have a suitable place to work. Chances are that if you ordinarily park your car on a busy city street, you'll be taking a big chance if you try to do major overhaul work there, even if you can reach the problem area from the sidewalk. A roomy garage or driveway will be far better. Make sure that there is sufficient room for you to move around the car, and that there's a place to put your tools while you're working. If it is necessary to run the car, be sure to leave the garage door completely open to assure ventilation.

In some cities, you can find "rental garages" where you can not only rent working space by the hour, but also suitable lifts, pits, and tools—and benefit from the owner's recommendations and advice in the bargain. If these are available to you, by all means take advantage of them.

If you're going to work outdoors, take weather conditions into consideration. Rain, snow, or other inclemencies will only hinder your efforts and, faced with such problems, you will be better off to put the work aside until a nicer day.

If you're going to work under the car, and are not dealing with the wheels or tires, small ramps that you drive the car up onto will raise either the front or rear end, and will provide more than enough clearance for you to get under the car in complete safety. When you work on a car in this position, always set the hand brake and chock the wheels for added safety. Chocks, or small blocks driven tightly under the wheels will keep the car from rolling.

Obviously, when you've got to work on the wheels, the tires, or brakes, you cannot simply roll the car up on ramps. For this type of work, we prefer a good-quality axle jack that operates on the screw principle. Set the jack to the desired height, raise the car, put the raised jack in position under the axle, and then lower the car onto the jack. The screw jack keeps the car safely elevated, and leaves the wheels free for your work. Any short cuts are not worth the risk involved and can result in total disaster.

Prepare for what you are going to do, also. If, for example, you plan to drain the crankcase of the old oil, make sure that you have a sufficiently-large pan to catch the drippings. Once you remove the drain plug, that black, messy oil is going to come gushing out, and you'd better be ready with something to catch it! When you remove parts, be certain that you have a suitable place to put them.

We've already suggested coveralls, and along with them, always wear an old cap or hat that will protect your head and hair, if you have any. Comfortably fitting clothes are better than tight, binding things that can get in the way when you're trying to maneuver a certain part. But loose, long sleeves can get caught, so be careful if your work clothes have such sleeves. It's also a good idea to keep a small supply of paper tags with strings and a sharp pencil handy. If you're disassembling something, these numbered labels can be invaluable when you start putting things together again.

Get the Names Right

In the Army, we used to call this "nomenclature," which is the military way of confusing things right from the start. While you can be perfectly clear yourself as to what a thing looks

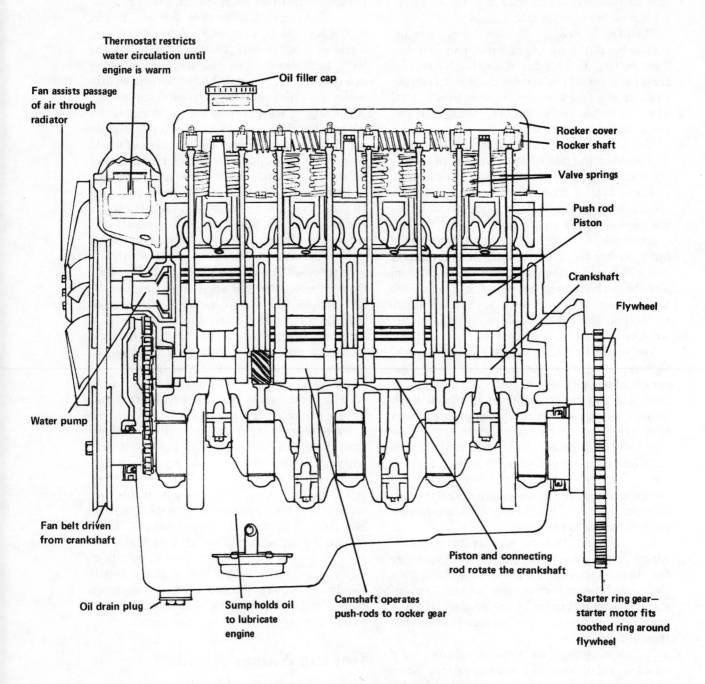

Thermostat restricts water circulation until engine is warm

Oil filler cap

Fan assists passage of air through radiator

Rocker cover
Rocker shaft

Valve springs

Push rod
Piston

Crankshaft

Flywheel

Water pump

Fan belt driven from crankshaft

Piston and connecting rod rotate the crankshaft

Oil drain plug

Sump holds oil to lubricate engine

Camshaft operates push-rods to rocker gear

Starter ring gear—starter motor fits toothed ring around flywheel

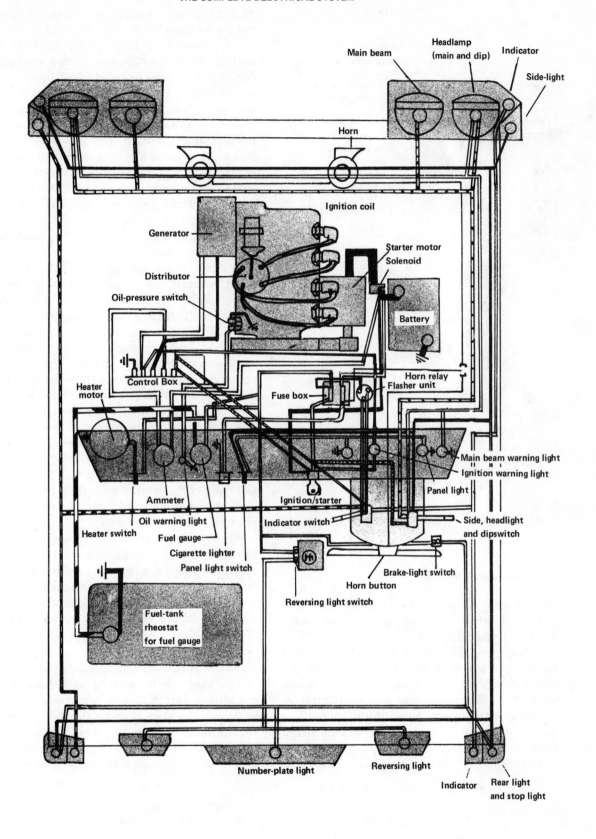

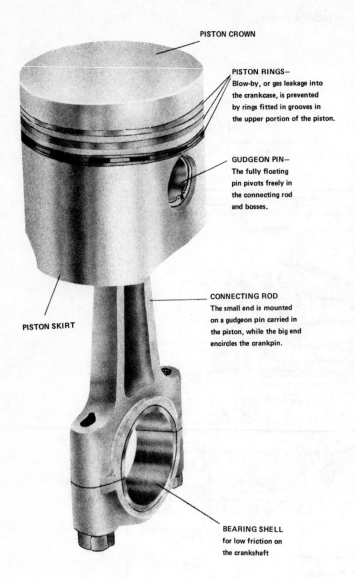

PISTON CROWN

PISTON RINGS—
Blow-by, or gas leakage into
the crankcase, is prevented
by rings fitted in grooves in
the upper portion of the piston.

GUDGEON PIN—
The fully floating
pin pivots freely in
the connecting rod
and bosses.

CONNECTING ROD
The small end is mounted
on a gudgeon pin carried in
the piston, while the big end
encircles the crankpin.

PISTON SKIRT

BEARING SHELL
for low friction on
the crankshaft

PISTON AND CONNECTING ROD

like, or what it does or where it goes, you just can't walk into an auto supply store and ask for a "whachamacallit" or a "thingamabob." In this book, we refer to parts by their correct names, and when we introduce a new part, we either describe or illustrate it so you'll know what it is. Whenever you are looking for or working with a part, name it (to yourself, if you're self-conscious about it) a half dozen times—*and* the parts that it connects to.

Most manufacturers of auto parts have their own coding. When you want to buy a replacement part for your car, you'll probably be faced with a wide and varied assortment. Air filters are typical—you'll find dozens available from each manufacturer. To buy a filter, consult the dealer's stock book or charts, look up the make, model and year of your car, and get the code number. Then select the right package from the dealer's shelf, and you're all set. Because of mass-production methods, you will probably find that several filters or other parts fit the same car. Don't be concerned about this, it's saving you money. If the manufacturers had to adhere to strict tolerances and make an individual part for each car, stocking them all would be prohibitive, and part costs much higher than they already are!

In some of the supply stores, the available stock is maintained on open display, and the responsibility for choosing the right package is your own. You take the package to a clerk at the cash register who simply wraps the package and takes your money. If you're buying an air filter, and simply grab a box from the shelf, you may find that you've gotten the wrong size or shape, and that you can't install it in your car. To find this out, you've opened the package, and as it can't be re-sold in that condition, you've bought it. Always check and double check before you make your selection. And, if you are still a bit unsure, it won't hurt to ask the sales clerk before he rings up the sale. You can never tell, he just might be able to confirm your selection.

While the information in this book will certainly be explicit, there is no such thing as too much knowledge. Always read the instructions printed on the manufacturer's package to make sure you know all that you can about the installation before you tear the package apart.

Jury-Rigging

You may not be able to find the exact replacement part that you require. If this happens, ask the shop to order the part for you. It can be there in from two days to a week, and you won't be compromising your installation. Never settle for a part that's "just as good," or "almost right." We've seen one extreme case where a man wasn't able to get the right size piston rings, ordered oversized rings instead, and had to have the cylinder walls bored to make up the difference!

Our philosophy is to adjust that which is adjustable, clean that which is dirty and, most of all, repair or replace that which is worn or malfunctioning. When we replace, we will replace with exact duplicate parts, and that means precisely what it says. Don't be lulled into accepting something that will only result in trouble later on, and cause you to re-do your work.

The same applies to tools. If a specific spanner is called for, wait until you can use the right tool and don't work "by guess and by gosh." You'll find, for example, that spark plugs must be installed to a certain pressure, usually fifteen pounds. To properly install the plugs, you need a torque wrench which will tell you how much pressure you are exerting. Most people don't have torque wrenches, and simply screw the plugs down as tightly as they can. It's a mistake.

Be practical! Suppose you have a dead cell in your battery. There is no practical, economical way that you can restore that cell to life, short of rebuilding the battery. And unless you are in the battery-building business, there's no way you can do that.

Instead, you must replace the battery. Once you have established the fact that the battery has one or more dead cells, replacing the battery is the only cure. One chap, in a massive effort to prove this wrong, drove a screw into the terminal of the last of his good cells, hacksawed the jumper apart, and then ran a cable to a second battery, tapping in to connect to its single live cell. It was a lot of work, and while it did operate after a fashion, proved ungainly and, in the final analysis, totally unworkable.

What makes a battery go bad? The battery consists of lead plates that are suspended in a solution of sulphuric acid. In use, the acid erodes the plates, causing lead flakes to fall to the bottom of the case. When a sufficient quantity of lead has dropped to form a bridge to the next adjacent plate (and they aren't all that far apart anyway), the battery develops an internal short circuit, and there goes the battery. The manufacturers do what they can to inhibit this flaking, including providing internal non-conductive blankets that keep the plates from shedding to a degree, but there is no cure.

Replacing a Part

Okay. A part has gone sour. What do you replace it with? We've told you to always replace with an exact duplicate replacement part. But what does an exact duplicate consist of? Take shock absorbers, for example. You'll find a dozen different kinds, all either exact duplicates or better. Should you go for the economy price? Or should you go all-out for the heavy-duty job that will outlast your car and help you haul super-heavy loads without bottoming out?

Spark plugs can be had at low prices, or you can find super-duper resistor types that will cost so much more that they *must* be better. Naturally, changing plugs is work, and you don't want to do more work than you have to, right? Aren't you better off, in the long run, to install the best in the hope that it will last longer and save you the extra work?

Not always.

I've always known that resistor spark plugs, for example, cost more than regular spark plugs, and therefore, considered them to be superior. Recently, I found out that the resistor element serves as a spark suppressor so that ignition noise won't be picked up by the car's radio. If you've never had resistor plugs in your car, and have no problem with noise in the radio, chances are that the spark suppressors are built into the receiver itself. Adding resistor plugs will net you nothing except a higher cost for the plugs.

It's essentially the same with those shocks. If most of your driving is over level ground, if you do not haul super-heavy loads, chances are that the ordinary "economy" shocks will suffice. If you find that your car does bottom out when you hit a pothole, you may want to invest a bit more for the heavier-duty units.

Chromium

It's a funny thing about chrome. It's bright and shiny, and sure does look pretty. We've also noticed that many of the replacement parts designed for under-the-hood use are now being offered in chrome, card-mounted and encased in protective blister-packed modules. These shiny gadgets are probably designed to attract the eye of the purchaser, and certainly succeed. But stop and think for a moment. Once the parts are installed and the hood is closed, they don't show. What's the point in paying all that extra money for chrome that can't be seen? Save your chrome money for outside the car, if that is your inclination.

Do it Right!

There's a joke I remember from my Boy Scout days—it takes only one man to tie a sailor's knot or a landlubber's knot. The difference between them is that it takes ten men to untie the landlubber's knot. Remember that everything you do on your car will have to be *undone* some day. If you tighten a part in place, always snug it down to proper torque values, and then keep in mind that your car vibrates when it operates. Go back a week later or so and check to see that the unit is still tight. It seems to be some kind of unwritten rule that, under vibration, screws and nuts always work themselves looser instead of tighter!

One of the things you're going to find is that parts installed under the hood will tend to get dirty and greasy. One of the first things you will have to do is clean and degrease these parts so they can be easily handled and examined. After you go to all the trouble of cleaning, you're going to be told to apply a light film of oil. This always shakes people. "I've just cleaned all the oil and grease *off* this blasted part! Why are you telling me to put more oil *on* it?"

Oil *does* make things oily—doesn't it? And oil picks up dirt and grease, too. But the oil also keeps things working the way they're supposed to, and will prevent the part from rusting.

But watch out with your lubricants. Where we specify a lube, we want the right lubricant used. Not any one you just happen to have around. Wherever we have metal rubbing on metal, we want a thin film of lubricant between them. But usually, where metal bears on metal in that fashion, there's pressure too, and the lubricant can be forced out of where it is needed. As a result, you can have surplus grease piled all around the place that it was forced and worked out of, and no lubricant at all where it is needed, at the metal-to-metal contact. Greases never work themselves *in*. However, there are ways to reduce the speed with which such lube losses can occur, and we'll tell you about these as we get to them.

Where This Book Stops

There are certain tasks in and around the car that we suggest you do not do. These are the jobs that require extensive equipment that is so specialized that you won't have access to it. We discuss those jobs anyway because by knowing what's involved, you will become an educated customer when you go to a mechanic and are less likely to be taken in by glib talk. Whenever you find that you require the services of a mechanic, always get a second diagnosis and a third if you feel this is necessary. You would do no less for your own body, were you talking to medical doctors or surgeons.

As for body work on the car. While we show you how to do the minor dent, ding, and body repair work, we suggest that the final coat of paint be applied by experts who are far-better equipped to do the job than you are. After all, while touch-up paints are indeed available at your local service store, you'll usually not be satisfied with the results. We're going to be teaching you some very valuable body-repair tricks, too.

Those touch-up colors can suffice, for example, if you get a scratch in the paint on the fender. You hit the scratch with some emery to feather-edge it, you apply a bit of primer, let that dry and then sand again to smooth the surface. Then you apply the touch-up paint, let it dry, and rub it down with some fine abrasive, apply a bit of wax, and keep your fingers crossed. But chances are that the paint on your car will be slightly sun-faded . . . the manufacturers of paint are rarely able to critically-control colors, and if you're fussy, this is not really the way to do it.

A deep bump in the fender can be filled with epoxy or fiberglass. When you've smoothed the whole thing down, you can mask the entire fender and spray it with anything from a spray gun to an aerosol can. But the fender still won't provide a very accurate match to the rest of the car, and the next stop will be to a commercial body-painter.

The Replacement Repair

While we show you how to repair body damage, sometimes the best way is to replace rather than repair. Many of today's body parts are interchangeable, so that a visit to your local junk yard might yield a completely replaceable fender and save you a lot of the hammer and tongs work otherwise called for.

To accomplish such a repair, you have to determine how the fenders are mounted to your car. If it's welded in place, forget it. The amount of work is far too excessive, and you'll do just as well to knock the dents out the hard way. But if the fenders are mounted with rivets or nuts and bolts, you've got little or no problem in removal and replacement. The chances are, however, that you won't get a replacement part in exactly the right color. So before the job can be called complete, painting one way or the other, will be needed.

One chap we know had purchased a brand-new car and soon thereafter got into a scrape that resulted in a slightly-dented left rear fender. The paint was chipped away to the bare metal, too. We advised him to get some paint over the dent at the very least, before rusting occurred, and having offered the advice, promptly forgot the matter until we saw the car again.

He had hired an artist to paint a Band-Aid over the dent, and to letter the word "ouch!" over that. It solved the problem of getting paint over the ding, not having to paint the whole car, and it exhibited a fine sense of humor that put a smile on the face of all who saw it.

It brought out an important point, too.

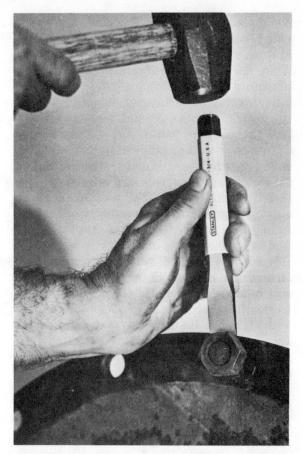

Disassembling body parts attached with bolts poses no problem, except that of loosening rusted nuts.

Can You Take It?

In doing *any* work on your car, don't lose your sense of humor. You are going to make mistakes. You're going to have to go over things maybe two or three times before you get them right. If you are cursed with a short temper, you can save yourself a lot of grief by calling it quits right now. If you're going to be working on your car *only* to save money, then the work will be "work" indeed, and maybe you should not be doing it.

But there are people who enjoy a good, hard job and don't mind a bit of grease on their hands. They know how to enjoy the work, and will profit from it.

For many people, manual work is a nice change from the mental efforts they must exert on their work-a-day jobs. But don't interpret this kind of "relaxation" in its literal sense.

When you're tired is not the time to work on your car. All you will do is become more tired. And when you're tired, you make mistakes. While the work is indeed relaxing, it is never a substitute for rest.

In this day of technology, many of us who enjoy working with our hands find ourselves in jobs that do not permit the satisfaction of handwork that our grandparents knew. Many engineers who are excellent craftsmen are not permitted to go near tools, and are restricted to their drawing boards. For people like that, owning a car offers the opportunity to work on it, and this provides almost as much pleasure as driving the automobile.

We have a friend who is a professional locksmith, a master locksmith in his own right, and became president of the world's largest locksmithing school. As good as this man is with his hands, his duties keep him deskbound. He makes executive decisions and directs the running of his company. But every once in awhile, he takes his coat off and goes down to the shop just to file a key or design a new lock. "The day I'm not allowed to work in my own shop," he says, "I'll close the doors!"

Control is required, too. A joke among mechanics is: "get a bigger hammer." But when a nut will not yield, this is not always the best way. When a nut holding a tailpipe is "frozen" in place, slamming the wrench with a hammer could easily damage structural members of the car and weaken them. The right way is to start with a penetrating liquid oil that should be applied liberally to and around the stubborn nut. Bang the nut a few times lightly to help the oil work its way into the rust, using capillary action. Under slight pressure, the nut should yield, if it does not, the nut must be sacrificed. We do this with a tool called a "nutcracker," which fits over the nut like a wrench. Tightening the threaded rod of the nut cracker drives a solid, sharp blade into the steel, causing the nut to break and separate so it can be removed. Naturally, when we replace the part, a new nut is used.

Now we're going to learn about tests we can make to evaluate a component before making a decision to replace it. In most cases, the only tools you will need are your head and your hands. Where special equipment is called for, it will be specified. So without further preliminaries, let's get started.

4
Examining and Testing Parts

There is no point in replacing components until we first establish that they are indeed faulty and in need of replacement. To determine that a fault exists, certain tests must be made. When you visit a doctor, he doesn't just toss you a pill. He checks your temperature, heart beat, blood pressure, and a half dozen other things; *then* he tells you what medication or corrective steps are required.

Testing allows us to narrow down all the possible things that might be causing the car to malfunction, so we have a better idea as to what the troubles might be. Happily, to a great extent, the car is self-analyzing. By listening and observing with care and intelligence, you can pretty well narrow things down without the need for extensive and expensive test equipment.

My Car Won't Start!

If, for example, the car cranks when you try to start it, but does not "catch," it could mean the carburetor is flooded. If you detect the odor of gasoline, the chances are that that is the problem and the easiest "cure" is simply to floor the accelerator and crank again.

If, on a second try, the engine still won't "catch," there's the possibility that no fuel is getting to the carburetor. If this happens, check to see whether or not there is any gasoline in the tank. Obviously, if the tank is empty, there's no way that fuel can get to the carburetor.

Barring this oversight, however, the testing process is relatively simple.

Begin by disconnecting the fuel line from the carburetor. Use a small wrench to loosen the coupling nut, and the line should quickly and easily come away from the carburetor.

With this line disconnected, attempt to start the car once again, feeding the gas. Naturally, the car will not start, for with the fuel line disconnected from the carburetor, no fuel can possibly get to the carb. However, this time we are not trying to start the car. We are making a test. Gasoline should come spurting out of the disconnected fuel line. Have an observer nearby to watch the fuel line and see if the gasoline appears as it should.

If it does, it indicates that the trouble is elsewhere, and we'll be getting to

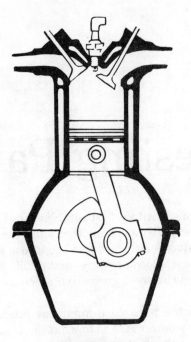

1 INDUCTION STROKE The inlet valve is open, the exhaust valve closed. The piston descends, inducing a flow of mixture. Soon after this stroke, the inlet valve is closed.

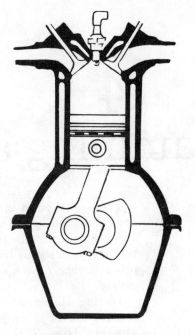

2 COMPRESSION STROKE Both inlet and exhaust valves are closed. The rising piston compresses the mixture in the combustion chamber and compression heat vaporises the mixture.

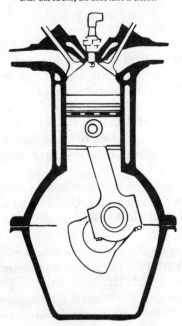

3 POWER STROKE Both valves remain closed. The compressed gas is ignited by a spark from the spark-plug. Expansion of burning gas drives the piston down. Exhaust valve opens.

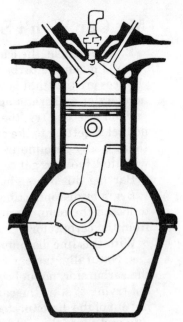

4 EXHAUST STROKE The inlet valve is closed, the exhaust valve is open. The piston rises to expel burnt gases, inlet valve opens, exhaust valve closes. Then the cycle begins over.

that later on. However, if *no* gasoline appears, trace the gas line back to its next junction, which will probably be the fuel filter. Disconnect the fuel line at that end and attempt to blow through it to see if the line is clogged. If you cannot get air through the line, certainly fuel won't go through, and you'll have to clean the line to remove the clog.

To clean the line, fill it with gasoline, straighten out a coat hanger wire and run that through the line a few times to break the clog. Finish the job by pushing a piece of plain lint-free cloth through the line.

If the line seems free, remove the fuel filter. Then attempt to start the car once again, and observe the gas line that is connected to the intake of the fuel filter.

If the line from the filter to the carburetor was clear, and if gasoline spurts from the line that was connected to the fuel filter's input, the problem is a clogged fuel filter. Correct the situation by changing fuel filters, reassemble the lines, and you are on your way.

Sometimes, however, it isn't all that simple. Continue to trace the line backwards, and you'll come to the fuel pump. Very often, a visual inspection can be most revealing. If the fuel pump is faulty, it will seem moist and greasy. Back in the old days, the fuel pump could be disassembled and faulty parts replaced. Usually, the part of a fuel pump that goes first is the actual pumping mechanism, called the "diaphragm." But you can't replace the diaphragm on a modern fuel pump, which is a sealed unit. What you can do is visit your local service shop and buy a new sealed unit for your own make and model of car, and install it in place of the old one.

Incidently, if your fuel pump is faulty, think back. Your car must have been trying to tell you for some time that a problem was developing, for when a fuel pump starts to go bad, the car loses pep, has trouble making it up the smallest of hills, and generally seems to act as though a tune-up is required.

As you can see, by following a logical, step-by-step procedure, we have checked out the car's fuel-feed system.

You may find, on disconnecting the fuel line that runs from filter to carburetor, that fuel is indeed being properly fed to the carburetor, but that the engine will still not catch. If you continue to crank the car, with everything connected up, you're going to flood the engine. Flooding is a condition that occurs when the cylinders are overfilled with fuel so the spark plugs cannot fire. Which leads us to another problem.

No Spark?

The spark plugs may *not* be firing. This changes the entire complexion of the problem from a fuel-connected one to an ignition one. Now we can rule out the battery as the cause of the problem, can't we? After all, the battery has sufficient power to crank the car. The battery supplies the voltage to operate the starting motor that causes the engine to rotate and crank. If the car is cranking, obviously, there's nothing wrong with the battery.

A good way to quickly check the ignition is to disconnect one of the spark-plug wires and hold it near the engine block. Have somebody crank the car by trying to start it. If the ignition up to the spark plugs is good, you'll get a zap of electricity and an arc at the end of the cable. This will occur each time that that particular plug should be firing. If you get the indication of electricity, it might be that the spark plugs are fouled. While you're making the tests called for, look at the fan at the front of the engine while the car is being cranked. Is the fan rotating each time? If it is not, this might indicate that one or more of the belts are loose. Check the belts to make sure that they are tight and in proper place, well-seated in the pulleys. A loose or broken belt could also be the cause of the troubles you are experiencing.

Gas-line Freeze

Unfortunately, because an engine runs hot, moisture can condense inside the fuel lines when the engine is turned off and is allowed to cool down. This moisture will settle in the low points of the line, as water is heavier than gasoline. What's more, water and gasoline are not miscible, and will remain separated. A "gas line freeze" means that water, which

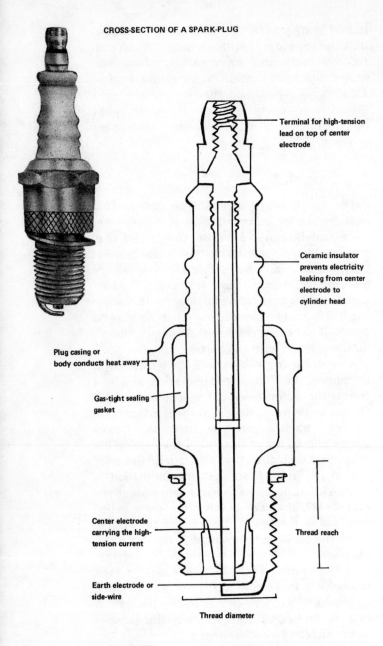

CROSS-SECTION OF A SPARK-PLUG

Terminal for high-tension lead on top of center electrode

Ceramic insulator prevents electricity leaking from center electrode to cylinder head

Plug casing or body conducts heat away

Gas-tight sealing gasket

Center electrode carrying the high-tension current

Thread reach

Earth electrode or side-wire

Thread diameter

has settled to the bottom parts of the gas line, has frozen and formed a blockage through which the gasoline cannot pass.

The object, of course, to get the car going again, is to eliminate the freeze and remove the water. The best and safest way to do this is to simply examine the gas line and disconnect those parts that appear low. These will be metal tubes, joined by couplings. Open the couplings and remove the tubing. Try to blow through the tubing to determine that ice has indeed formed and is forming a block.

Take the frozen length of tubing into a warm area where it will quickly thaw and allow you to breathe through it. Do not try to accelerate the thawing process with heat or flame, as there may still be gasoline vapors in the line, or even trapped in the line. When the ice has melted, and all the water has been removed, pour a bit of alcohol through the tube, as alcohol is a desiccant and will remove the last vestiges of moisture.

Remember, however, that the tubing is now warm, and you are going to take it back into the cold. More moisture can condense on the walls. Prevent this by corking both ends of the tube until you are ready to install it once again.

This problem of moisture in the gasoline lines is a crucial one that airplane pilots know about. You take a nice warm day followed by a cool night, and a condensate of water will form on the inner walls of the gas tank. This can drop to the bottom of the tank, in the form of water. One of the pre-flight checks that all pilots perform is to "drain the sumps" by opening a valve under each of the wing tanks to let the accumulated water flow out, leaving only gasoline in the tank. A smart pilot will also have his tanks "topped off" at the end of each day's flying, so there is no room for moisture to collect.

The driver of an automobile cannot easily do all of these things, and therefore, other steps must be taken. In areas and time of suddenly dropping temperatures, we recommend the addition of "dry gas" which is sold at most service stations. You pour a can into each tankful of gas, and the moisture that would have collected will be desiccated and you will not experience these problems. It's the old "ounce of prevention," all over again.

The entire purpose of this discussion was to make the point that there is nothing mysterious about the automobile or its engine. A smart mechanic is like a detective who examines his available clues and then draws a conclusion. He then applies certain specific tests to verify his conclusion before he sets about making repairs. Keep in mind that your malfunctioning car *did* work once, until something went sour. Locate and repair or replace the malfunctioning part, and the car will work again.

As you can see, the tests that we advocate do not require fancy test apparatus. What they do require is common sense, careful thought, and enough restraint to keep you from tearing off into ten different directions all at once. There are so many things that might be wrong with a car, that you have to spend some time just "head scratching" before you dig in. Just saying, "My car doesn't work," won't help, if you just stop there. The smart driver will slip behind the wheel and figure out the why's and wherefore's for himself. In a short time, you will learn to isolate many problems without even thinking twice. In fact, you've already got a head start. You wouldn't change the tires because the car doesn't start, would you? Always be alert to symptoms, the signs of trouble that can lead you to where the trouble lies.

Overheating

Suppose the car seems to overheat constantly. This is an indication of trouble in the cooling system. It can be caused by a number of problems, all of which are relatively easy to check. Because a car's engine creates a lot of friction, check the oil level first. If there is not sufficient oil in the crankcase, overheating is sure to result.

Next, check the level of coolant in the radiator. Should the level drop, this too can cause overheating. If the level is obviously very low, it might also indicate a leak in the cooling system, which must be repaired at once. Finally, check to see that the fan is operating properly. If all of these are in good shape, it may indicate a faulty water pump, a faulty thermostat, or it may just be that the belt driving the water pump is loose or broken. All of these except for the thermostat can be checked and examined visually.

If you find that the water level is low, add additional water when the engine has cooled. Never add cold water to an overheated engine, or you will risk cracking the engine block due to thermal shock. If you add water and it drops again, this might indicate a leaky hose. As you can see, we trace a fault by careful analysis, and correcting the fault will correct the problem.

Tire Wear

There are steps of a preventive nature that we can take, too. Let's talk about tires, for a moment. Automobile tires have deep treads which are designed to grip the road. After many miles of driving, the tire treads will exhibit signs of wear. If the wear appears to be equal on the tires' surfaces, the only thing you have to do is rotate the tires periodically. If the tires seem to be wearing more at the insides than the outer edges, it indicates that you have been over-inflating them, probably because you prefer the feel of a "harder" ride. If, on the other hand, the maximum wear is at the outer edges, your tires have been under-inflated. If the tires on one side of the car indicate more wear than the tires on the other side, this indicates incorrect camber or toe-in. Your own mechanic can best correct problems such as that.

You see, wear is never entirely even on tires. By rotating the tires, even if they do not seem to require it, we assure ourselves that we're preserving tire life, which is precisely what we are doing.

But incorrect camber or toe-in can cause the tires to run in a pigeon-toed fashion. If you consider this for a moment, you'll realize that when a tire operates like this, instead of running directly forward, more wear takes place than should normally occur. While you could balance the wear by rotating the tires, you are not solving the basic problem, which is that the tires wear too rapidly, reducing your economy.

What few people realize, however, is that a certain amount of camber and toe-in is necessary, for a tire at rest aligns itself with the car differently than a tire that is rotating at high speed. Correct toe-in is therefore a compromise. If we were to vastly improve tire life, we'd want a toe-in that varied with the car's speed. While we have the technology to do this, the cost would be far more than we were trying to save.

But a car with a bad case of camber or toe-in is something like a Russian troika, which is a carriage or sleigh drawn by three horses. One pulls forward, another is directed slightly left, another slightly right. It's a totally inefficient system, with only one-third of the horsepower operating at peak efficiency.

Other preventive measures can be taken to keep small problems from becoming big ones. Here are some easy ones.

Cleaning

The first step in cleaning any automotive components is to remove all film and caked-on or dried lubricants. But before you start, be warned that many of the solvents that will attack and remove petro products will also attack rubber and plastics which are petroleum derivatives. Be very careful that you do not get oil, grease, or such solvents on plastic or rubber parts. If you do, remove the solvents at once, or they'll render the rubber parts useless.

One of the most common grease-cutters, of course, is gasoline. Although this is highly volatile and dangerous to use, many mechanics prefer to soak a dirty part in a tub of gasoline to soften the caked-on grime, thereby saving themselves some of the hard work. However, there are commercial degreasers that will accomplish the same thing without the danger of fumes and vapors. You'll find such products at your local auto supply store, and they're nice to have on hand.

Having softened the grease, swish the component in the liquid to wash away as much as you can. Rub it with your hand, then wipe it with a lint-free rag to get off as much of the grease as possible. Now place the part in a second bath of the same degreaser which will remove most of the additional dirt. The reason for the two-step process is to keep the second bath from getting as dirty as the first.

Here's a money-saving hint: after you've finished cleaning all your parts, throw the first (dirtiest) bath away, then slowly pour the liquid from the second bath into a suitable container, which you can store for use as a first bath next time you work. You'll notice that the sludge settles to the bottom, and you can stop pouring before the sludge gets into your container.

After cleaning, completely dry the part and examine it. If it is not cleaned to your complete satisfaction, a wire brush will help dislodge any residual grease. Make sure the part is completely clean and bright.

Now that you've got all the grease off, you will have to remove any traces of the degreaser chemical. We prefer to use ordinary household alcohol for this, as the alcohol takes the chemical off and acts as a desiccator, too. It removes all water and the alcohol dries quickly, leaving the part ready for the next step.

Because there is now no lubricant left on the part, it will rust quickly unless you take steps to protect it by applying lubricant. You can either spray light oil from an aerosol can, or you can dip the entire part in a bath of oil. Make sure all surfaces are coated, then put the part aside on a stack of old newspapers so the excess oil can drain off.

To clean rubber parts, use a rubber restorative. This will clean and refresh the rubber, and will not damage it. In most cases and as a general rule, since rubber does have a limited life, you'll want to change the rubber part rather than attempt to restore it.

Should you remove spark plugs to clean and re-gap them, always replace the small metal washer that seats between the plug and its threaded hole. Once these washers are compressed by the spark plug, they cannot be reused, and must be replaced. As they cost only pennies, this is not usually a problem.

Carbon

Some components, such as your spark plugs, will generate great heat. In addition to the build-up of grease on the body of the plug, carbon may build up at the terminals.

This carbon will not always yield to the usual cleaning process. If you have access to a sand-blasting machine designed for this work, by all means take advantage of it. You simply insert the plug into a rubber grommet, and a spray of sand will remove all carbon deposit. If you do not have such a device, you may be able to purchase a spark-plug file and by dressing the terminals with this file, you can remove all carbon, leaving the plug ready for re-gapping and installation.

Under the Valve Cover

If you have occasion to remove the valve

cover from the engine, the first steps will be a clean-up. Start by cleaning the cover itself, inside and out. Pay particular attention to removing the traces of the old gasket material from the lip of the cover. You can scrape most of this away with a dull knife, and then degrease the cover and clean it thoroughly.

Now get to work on the top of the engine block and head cover, removing the oil and grease with towelling. Use your knife to get all the old gasket cement and gasket off, too. Leave the surface clean and bright. If you leave any traces of the old gasket on the head cover or inside the valve cover, you can be sure that you will develop oil leaks when your reassembly is completed.

There is no way at all that you can salvage the old gasket. It must be continuous and in one piece, if a proper seal is to be made, and rest assured that the old gasket will have been compressed to a point where it cannot properly function again.

A new gasket to fit the year, make and model of your car will have to be purchased. This will be furnished in a sealed plastic pack, and should be left in the pack right up to the last minute, when you're ready to install it.

There are many schools of thought on the proper way to install the gasket, but we prefer to apply a continuous bead of gasket cement to the valve cover and then seat the gasket in the cover, making sure all the mounting holes line up. Allow this to dry thoroughly before proceeding.

Then place the cover in position on the head cover, align the holes, press down firmly, and hand-tighten the bolts in place. Using the correct wrench, tighten the bolts one at a time, a little at a time, until all bolts are fast. This keeps the cover from bending or warping. Now check the oil level, turn on the engine, and run the car for at least five minutes, to make sure there are no oil leaks.

One of the reasons for changing the valve-cover gasket is that you may have noticed some oil leakage from around the cover. Changing this gasket will stop such oil leakage, giving you better oil economy and helping keep your engine cleaner. If you see oil leakage of this type, the work is well worth the effort.

Test First

I'm sure you've heard the story of the girl who washed her hair, not because it was dirty, but because it was Saturday. Many people follow such rules of thumb when it comes to servicing their cars. However basic these rules are, they are not always economical—or advisable. Although it's been conceded that modern lubricants can perform well beyond the prescribed period, people still change their oil— whether it needs changing or not—every five or six thousand miles. While we do not recommend that you run the car until the oil turns to sludge, you should get more than five thousand miles out of any good grade of oil.

By the same token, the car should not be tuned-up simply because it has run a given number of miles. It should be tuned up when it *needs* a tune-up. The things that indicate the need for a tuning include hard starting, rough idling, or dieseling, i.e., the after-run that can occur after you turn off the ignition. If the car runs rough, becomes sluggish or lacking in pep, a tune-up might be needed. But if the car is behaving well, starts easily, idles smoothly and has all the pep it ever did have, why bother with the costly tune-up? Save your money until a tune-up is called for, then have it done.

This sort of advice might upset the professional mechanic who sees his income dwindling as a result. Asking him if your car needs an oil change or a tune-up usually elicits the pat answer "How long since the last one?" And if you come up with the right number, he smiles . . . and starts counting your money. However, we aren't writing this book for the mechanic. It's for you. We want to show you how to get the most out of your car-care dollar.

Sometimes a repair job is not essential to cure an ailing automobile. Our car has valve lifters, called tappets. Periodically, they start making a clicking noise under the hood. This can be corrected by having them adjusted and having the bad ones replaced, and it's certainly a job we would assay for ourselves. However, getting around to it is the big problem. Time has just not permitted it. Because the valve cover must be removed, then cleaned up, and the gasket changed at the same time, we've been putting the job off to a rainy day.

So, to eliminate the noisy clicking, we would start the engine, let it warm up, and then pour a can of oil additive to the crankcase. The clicking would stop, or would muffle sufficiently so that we could continue to use the car—until we got our sleeves rolled up.

Sometimes, you are perfectly capable of doing a job, yet would prefer to pay somebody else to do it. It's worth the cost not to have to spend a Sunday out at the car.

Be careful, too. Many of the parts on your car were designed to be cleaned and replaced, rather than changed. In recent years, a lot of car manufacturers have been providing what are called "permanent" air filters. These are made of a breathable, cellulose plastic. When they become clogged with dirt, you are supposed to remove the filter, wash it thoroughly, and then replace it. If you did not know about this, you might remove the filter, throw it away, and replace it with a far less valuable replacement element that you bought at a store. Always check carefully before making a "throw-away" decision.

Hoses

In an up-coming chapter, we're going to be talking about the hoses that are used to conduct fluids from one part of the car to another. These hoses come in several different types and sizes. Changing them is a simple matter, too.

What happens is that after constant exposure to engine heat, or the unending flow of liquids through them, they either become soft and spongy, or they embrittle. In either case, they must be changed before they rupture and spill their contents on the roadway. Considering the high cost of coolants, it's worth replacing a hose before the coolant is lost.

Usually, the hoses leading to the inlet and outlet of the car's heater are simply standard high-pressure hoses. You buy the length you require, remove the old hose, and slip the new hose into place. Examine the clamps, and if they are rusted, you may want to replace them also, while you are changing the hose. When you get the old hose off, clean the nozzles to which it was attached, using a wire brush. Apply a bit of petroleum jelly to the nozzles to help slip the hoses on more easily.

The hoses leading from the radiator to the engine block are usually preformed and shaped, according to the needs of the individual car. Purchase these in advance of the work, and you'll have little or no difficulty in making the installation.

Other Tips

While our primary purpose is to show you how to work on and with the car, to the condition you got it from the manufacturer, there are some helping-hand, car-saving aids that the manufacturers did not see fit to install. One typical example concerns the differential, that large blob of metal located centrally on the car's rear axle. Inside this is a collection of gears that permit the rear wheels to counter-rotate so you can make a turn without having the rear tires skid. Periodically, you should check the level of the lubricant in the differential. You do this by removing the large, screw-in plug, inserting your finger, and then withdrawing it. But one of those times, before you put the cap back in place, attach a small Alnico magnet to the steel plug. The magnetism will hold the plug and magnet together, and at the same time withdraw the small abraded metal chips that might otherwise be circulating in the lubricant. Periodically, remove the plug and wipe away the metal collection, then replace the plug. You'll be quite impressed with the quantity that is removed.

In the days of the early automobile batteries, before the new fancy plastics were developed, the manufacturers used a soft, tar-like material to cover the battery tops. On a warm day, you could press your thumb nail into this stuff and leave an impression. What we used to do was drive a copper penny into the tar right alongside the anode terminal. All the corrosion and the resultant white material that usually collected on the anode, would collect on the penny instead. This "sacrificial anode" could then be removed and tossed away (it only cost a cent!) and replaced with a new, shiny penny.

You can't drive a coin into today's modern battery, but you can purchase a special battery terminal connector that has a penny mounted on it. If you can find one of these at your local dealer, by all means install it. That penny is there for more than just "good luck!"

Our next chapter will discuss the wheels and shocks, and we'll tell you more of those things that can save your car and save you money.

5
The Wheels, Brakes, and Shock Absorbers

Those things that support the vehicle off the ground are as basic yet as critical as any of the other components of an automobile. Fortunately, many of these parts are self-analyzing. This means that when something is wrong or is going wrong you'll know it, and without having to make extensive or exhaustive tests.

For instance, let's consider a flat tire. You *know* the tire is flat, just by looking at it! You know what must be done about it, too. You set the brakes, jack the car, remove the tire and put on the spare. But there are other indications of tire problems.

Tire Pressure

If a tire is "low," chances are that you'll also be able to tell this simply by observation. A better way, however, is with a tire pressure gauge. You can buy one at your auto supply store for well under a dollar, and it should be used often—especially before starting on any long trip. As we know, tire wear can be attributed to improper inflation, and we don't want to replace tires any more often than we have to. By using the tire pressure gauge, you eliminate guesswork. You will know exactly what the tire air pressure is, and if it isn't right for your car, you can adjust it.

There are several ways to tell that a tire is "low." The best way of course, is to use a tire pressure gauge, which will tell you exactly the air pressure in your tire. Usually, however, this is used as a means of determining what you already suspect. How can you suspect a tire? For one thing, if you do *not* have power steering (which will compensate automatically) you will feel the car "pulling" toward the side with the low tire. Another indication is that the tire seems flatter than usual, and the side walls of the tire bulge more than they should. However, the new radial tires are supposed to bulge a bit, so don't let that throw you. Your surest, safest test is always with a tire pressure gauge.

Too many people rely on the gauges that are a part of the air service at their local service stations. They dial up the pressure they desire, and then fill the tire until the air stops flowing. Unfortunately, these gauges are rarely even close to accurate. All they really provide is a false sense of security. You are far-better off to set the pump gauge a bit higher than you really need, and check the tire pressure with your own gauge, as you fill the tire.

How much pressure should you use? Your car most probably came equipped with a manual that will indicate this. If you no longer have the manual, check the inside of your car's glove compartment. Many manufacturers affix a small label there, indicating such information. There are two tire pressures that you will be concerned with. When a car has been standing idle for awhile, the air in the tires will cool down and contract, thereby reducing the pressure by several pounds. When the car has been operating, the tires and the air inside them will heat up. This causes the internal pressure to increase. Obviously, we do not want to inflate a cold tire to the maximum pressure. This would result in overinflation when the tire heats up.

Another rather interesting tire test that is easy to make, is the ten-cent tread test. Hold an ordinary dime so the date shows above your thumb. Now insert the dime into the tire treads so the rim of the dime bottoms against the rubber. The tire tread should be of sufficient height that you cannot read the date. If you can, the tire tread is dangerously low, and the tire should be replaced or retreaded.

Retreads

What about retreads? You probably know that you can save a good deal of money by buying retreads, but are they a good investment? They are, if you know what to look for.

Make sure that the "retread" tire you are buying is not simply "regrooved." In retreading, new rubber is added to and firmly bonded to the old tire surface. In a regrooved tire, hot rotary dies are pressed into the remaining rubber on the tire, so that new, deeper grooves are cut into it. Regrooved tires, having less rubber, are not as safe.

A retreaded tire, on the other hand, is as good as the old tire's wall casing. You have to be very careful to inspect the old tire walls very carefully. Make sure there are no cut marks and no deep abrasion marks.

The fact is that a cut in the wall of a tire is harder to spot than a bruise. Rubber, of which tires are made, is very flexible, and a cut will usually (if it's a small one) close right up. The damage is there, but you can't see it.

A bruise, on the other hand, is easy to spot. It's a scrape. It's a damage that isn't easy to hide. You'll see tire bruises when you run your car up against a curb. Of course, tire bruises aren't as damaging as cuts or slashes usually, but they look ugly, and can erode the surface rubber, and weaken the tire wall. Once a bruise occurs, there's nothing you can do to replace the worn-away rubber, but you can eliminate the ugliness by applying a tire-dressing compound, available at your local auto supply store. It won't help the tire's life once the damage has been done, but the tire will, at least, look nicer.

If you think you see a cut mark on the casing wall, do not hesitate to flex the tire to confirm your findings. Next, use a flashlight to examine the inside of the casing. Watch for plug marks that would indicate where the tire might have been repaired. Do not hesitate to reject a tire that you suspect was damaged in its earlier life.

Time to Rotate

Because of the camber or toe-in of most cars, there will be an imbalance applied to the car's tires. To compensate for this, we rotate the tires from front to back and from side to side. This provides more even wear and gives you a longer useful life expectancy from your tires. Rotating the tires is an easy job that you can do yourself.

Chances are that when you bought your car, you received an instruction manual that will indicate the method of tire rotation. In general, however, the left front becomes the right rear, the right front becomes the left rear, and the two rear tires move diagonally to their opposite corners.

The tires should be rotated approximately every ten thousand miles, for best results, and any signs of uneven wear should be noted, and checked for cause.

When you rotate your tires, you'll want your wheels re-balanced anyway. No wheel is perfectly balanced when it is made, and compensating weights have to be added in the right amount and at the right places.

This must be done by a mechanic, who will remove the old weights, and place the tire on a spindle with a bubble level at the center. Then he will add the weights at the tire's rim to move the bubble to the center. The weights are then clinched in place.

Balancing the tire in this fashion assures you that the tire will rotate evenly on its hub, with no "heavy" sides.

Hubcaps

To many people, the hubcaps represent a cosmetic addition to the car, but this is not exactly true. While the hubcaps make the car look nicer, of course, they also have a very practical function, that of keeping dirt and grease away from the lug nuts that hold the wheel to the car. If you lose a hubcap, replace it as soon as you can, and until you can replace it, pack some heavy grease over the lug nuts. Should you have to change a tire before the cap is replaced, all you will need to do is wipe away the grease first. The lug nuts will come away easily, not having to thread themselves over grit and rust. After you put the hubcap back, always apply one of those little covers over the valve stem. It will help to protect the delicate valve mechanism, and save you some grief in the future.

Don't Forget the Spare

While you may be willing to accept the problems of tire maintenance, it usually takes a fairly dedicated driver to check the spare tire each and every time. While it only means opening the trunk once in awhile to make sure that the spare will be ready when it is needed, too many people are prone to forget that spare tire until it *is* needed, and then it is sometimes too late.

We found a handy little device that can be easily installed. It consists of a rubber hose with fittings at either end. You start by punching a small round hole (there is a method to this madness, see below) in the body of the car near the trunk lid, on the same side as the spare tire is located. Attach one end of the hose through the car's body, tightening the nut to compress the rubber seal and prevent leakage. The other end screws into the valve stem on the spare tire. Know what this little thing does for you? It permits you to check the air in the spare *without opening the trunk*. Look for one at your local auto supply store. You'll be glad that you did.

To punch a hole in the body of the car, begin by using a center punch and a hammer, which will

With its head and point heat-treated, the center punch is designed to mark metal and punch holes in metal and other materials.

put a small, sharp dent in the body. Now put a small-size drill bit (maybe 1/16th inch) in your power drill, and place the bit point in the center punch mark. Drill this "pilot" hole through the car's body.

Now use a slightly larger drill, perhaps ⅛ inch to enlarge the hole a bit, and then a ¼-inch drill to make it still larger. Let me explain the reason for all of this up to this point.

If you do *not* center punch first, the drill will skid and twist about instead of biting into the metal, and you'll not make the hole precisely where you wanted it. What's more, you'll only damage the car's paint.

If you do not gradually increase the drilled hole sizes, the hole you make will be out-of-round.

If the final hole you require is ⅜ inch or less, use a hand-tapered reamer to enlarge the hole. Then, when the hole is of the size you need, use a one-inch twist drill to remove the burrs from both sides of the metal. A few light twists with your hand will do it.

To make a half-inch hole, use a device called a "Chassis punch" (these come in all sizes from ½ inch to two inches diameter). The chassis punch has a punch, a die, and a large, threaded screw. You place the screw through the punch, then place it through the hole in the car's body, and thread the die at the other end. Now use a wrench to tighten the screw which draws the die through the body of the car and into the punch. The result is a nice, clean hole.

What About Flat Tires?

The next question that must come up is, should you repair your own flat tires? The answer is no. While you may very well understand how this is done, and probably *can* do it yourself, just watch your mechanic the next time he repairs one for you. He has special tools for dismounting and remounting the tire, and can do it a lot faster and better than you can, with a lot less work. Leave that job to him.

In recent years, there's been a handy device that belongs in your car. It's aerosol powered, contains a rubbery gook along with sufficient air to re-inflate your tire, and when you get a flat, you simply screw this thing to the valve stem and gook and air rushes into the tire. The air carries the chemical to the damage and, if it is a small enough hole, will plug it. This will get you to the nearest gas station where the mechanic can check and fix the tire properly. These things are worth the space in anybody's trunk.

We recently had a funny option offered to us. Our car hit a pothole, and soon thereafter, the tire went flat. We changed to the spare, and stopped in at a local garage. "Tire's flat," we offered. The mechanic added some air to inflate the tire, then dunked it in water. Soon he located the leak. The pothole had bent the wheel rim, and a tracing of bubbles was escaping between the raised bead of the tire and the bent rim.

"Hmmph," he hmmphed. "We can either put a new wheel rim under the tire, or we could put in a tube." It was a tubeless tire, and we hated to add a tube to it, but we asked anyway. "How much is a new rim?" He looked up. "Five bucks." "And how much for a tube?" "Five bucks."

We did a little head scratching, spotted a mechanic's five-pound maul nearby, and borrowed it for a moment. Three shots on the wheel rim straightened the rim sufficiently so that immersing the tire once again revealed no air leakage at all. "What do I owe you for the loan of the hammer?" The mechanic looked at me with a big grin. "Nothing, Mac—I just learned a new trick!"

Brakes

The brakes do not stop the car. They stop the wheel, and the wheel stops the car. While a lot of things can go bad with brakes, most of them are again of the self-analyzing kind and relatively easy to correct.

You may notice that your brake is low. In other words, when you step on the brake pedal, the car travels a good distance before the pedal bottoms out and brings the car to a halt. If you are concerned about this, you have a right to be. After all, what would happen if you stepped on the brake and the pedal went all the way to the floor boards but didn't stop the car? You'd be in big trouble! This does happen, and it indicates that a leakage has occurred in the hydraulic lines and the fluid has exited—in essence, you have no brakes.

When you notice that the brakes are low, you will want to add additional hydraulic fluid to the master cylinder. The master cylinder is a cylindrical object with a plunger rod emerging from one end, and this is coupled to the brake pedal in such a way that when the brake pedal is depressed, you will see the push rod of the cylinder move into the cylinder. It emerges when the brake pedal is released. To locate it, simply observe the nether end of the brake pedal and you will see that, through a series of linkage arms which provide mechanical advantage, the brake is connected to this cylinder which is usually mounted in the engine compartment under the hood, generally (depending on the car) on the firewall or bulkhead.

A tube or tubes extend from the master cylinder and will be connected to the various brake cylinders (one at each wheel), which are used to actuate the brake linings against the brake drums when the cylinders are activated. Here's how it works:

You step on the brake, compressing the hydraulic fluid in the master cylinder. This in turn escapes under pressure to the various brake cylinders, operating them. They cause the brake lining to rub against the brake drum, and this causes the wheel to stop rotating, the car to stop.

If air gets into this fluid, the brakes will have

MAIN PARTS OF A DISC BRAKE

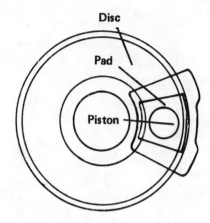

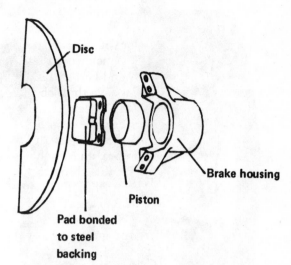

DISC AND PAD Because only a little of the disc area is covered by the caliper, the disc is quickly cooled by air. Water is also quickly spun away

MAIN COMPONENTS The caliper casting is made in halves, each containing a cylindrical housing, a piston and a pad, which are bolted together

A DISC BRAKE IN ACTION

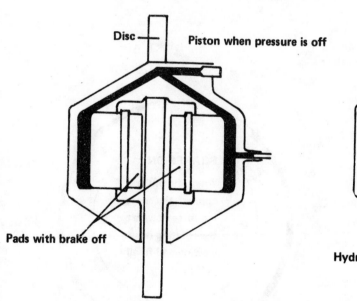

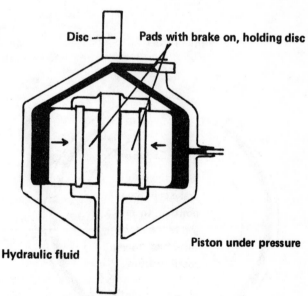

OFF When the brakes are not in use, the pressure on the friction pads is released.

ON When the brake is applied, hydraulic pressure forces the pistons to press the friction pads against the faces of the disc to brake the car

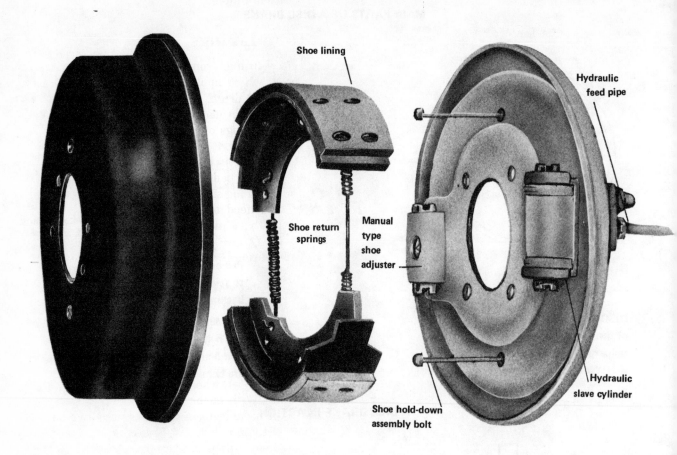

Shoe lining

Hydraulic feed pipe

Shoe return springs

Manual type shoe adjuster

Hydraulic slave cylinder

Shoe hold-down assembly bolt

BRAKE DRUM   **SHOE**   **BACK PLATE**

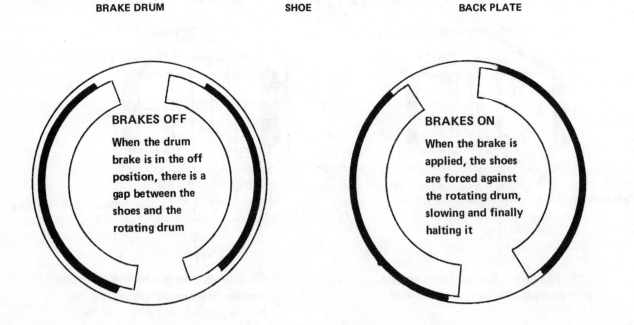

BRAKES OFF

When the drum brake is in the off position, there is a gap between the shoes and the rotating drum

BRAKES ON

When the brake is applied, the shoes are forced against the rotating drum, slowing and finally halting it

a "spongy" feel instead of a firm, positive action. If the fluid is low or has been lost due to a crack or hole, you will have no braking power at all. In the top of the master cylinder is a small, threaded plug. Remove this plug to check the fluid level and, if it is low, add additional brake fluid. When you have added sufficient fluid to bring it up to the "full" line inscribed on the unit, replace the plug, and then vigorously pump the brake pedal to circulate the fluid. Open the plug and fill it again, if necessary. This may have to be done a few times. After such a treatment, the brakes usually come up to the level where they are supposed to be.

The brake action as felt through the brake pedal should be crisp and smooth. If you press down and the pedal feels "soft" or "bouncy," you may have air trapped in one of the hydraulic fluid lines leading to the individual wheel cylinders, or in a cylinder itself. If this is the case, the lines have to be bled.

To do this, remove the individual hoses from the wheel cylinders, working on a single cylinder at a time. Have somebody depress the brake, and the fluid will spurt out of the hose. Any entrapped air will bubble out at the same time. While your friend keeps the brake depressed, replace the hose. When you have done this for all four wheels, refill the master cylinder as previously described.

While you are checking the brakes, have somebody stand in back and check the brake lights. Every time you step on the brakes, the brake lights should come on. If they do not, it might indicate a burned-out lamp, which should be replaced. When both lights fail to function, and the lamps are not burned out, first check the fuse to see that it is in good order. (See page 66.) If it is, the trouble might well be in the brake light switch.

If the switch is bad, simply buy a replacement. Begin removing the old switch by loosening the screws that hold the wires to the switch terminals. The wires should then come away quite easily. Now rotate the body of the switch so the nut which holds it in place will loosen. You can then remove the mounting nut, take out the old switch, and put the new one into place. Replace the nut, tighten it, and then put the wires back on the proper terminals. It's really that simple!

Brake Linings

Brake linings consist of an asbestos-like material which applies the stopping pressure to the brake drum. As a car is used, the brake linings will abrade and will wear thinner and thinner. Linings once were held to the brake shoe by rivets, but now almost all are bonded in place with adhesive.

A squealing sound when you apply the brake is a pretty good sign that the linings are well-worn and need to be replaced. If this is not done, the bare metal exposed after the lining wears away will abrade on the brake drum and cause additional wear that will be expensive to restore.

The easiest way to check for worn brake linings is to listen to your car for that tell-tale squeal. To check the linings visually, however, it is necessary to remove the wheel. So it would be a good idea to have the brake linings checked along with the wheels every ten thousand miles (when you rotate the tires, for example). With the brake cover out of the way, you will be able to see the linings, and how much of them is left.

If the old linings are badly worn, drop in at your local auto supply store for new brake linings, which come in pairs. There are two supplied for each wheel. While it's an easy enough and interesting job to tackle, there are certain inspection procedures you should perform before you start installing the new linings.

Once you have removed the wheel and the wheel hub cover, which is a seamless metal shell, remove the cotter pin from the axle and lift off the wheel drum, thereby exposing the brake system so that the old brake linings are visible. Observe the system of springs and actuators that work with the brake shoe. Feel the inside of the brake drum to see if it needs refacing. If the drums have become scored and in need of refacing, take the car to a competent mechanic. This is a job you cannot do, and if he's going to do that part of the job, he may as well replace the linings also.

1 The bleeder nipple—which on drum brakes is on the backplate, or on the caliper of disc brakes—must be free of all grease and dirt before the rubber or plastic tube is attached.

2 The free end of the tube must be completely immersed throughout the bleeding process in a jar containing some hydraulic fluid. If air is allowed to be drawn back into the system, the work will have to be begun again.

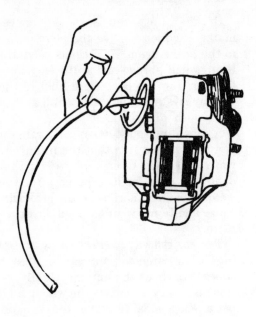

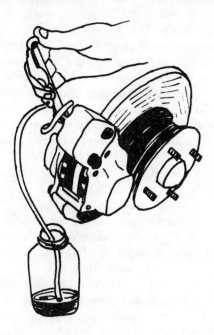

BLEEDING THE BRAKES

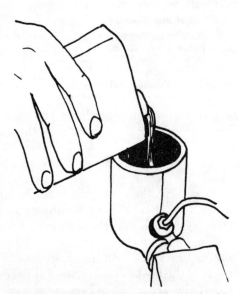

3 After bleeding each brake, the reservoir should be topped up (this is found in the engine compartment) with the correct kind of fluid for your car. Great care must be taken to prevent the fluid becoming contaminated with water, dirt, grease or anything else.

4 In bleeding and checking the master cylinder reservoir, always make sure the small air hole in the top of the cap is free of dirt before replacing.

To reface the brake drums, they are placed on a special lathe, and are turned down to remove sufficient metal so that the score marks are eliminated.

If your drums do not need refacing, but your linings do need a change, you can do the work yourself. Simply remove the old linings, install the new ones, reassemble the brake system, replace the wheel, and the job is done.

Sometimes, you'll find that the linings have worn, but not enough to require replacement. Still, the brakes seem a bit low.

You can adjust the brakes. An inexpensive brake-adjusting tool is inserted in a slot in the wheel, and worked up and down to raise the space between lining and drum. Check this work by occasionally spinning the wheel. You want the lining to be in sufficient contact with the drum so that while no pressure is exerted on the drum with the brake at rest, there will be sufficient drag to keep the wheel from rotating freely.

Be careful not to overdo the adjustment, however. This is not a substitute for changing the linings.

Shock Absorbers

You know, of course, that your car has springs which keep you from bouncing hard as the car moves over the road. But you may not know that any spring must flex in both directions. It compresses, then it expands, and then it compresses again to a lesser degree, expands a bit less, and finally, settles back to the norm. If that were all there was to a car's suspension, you would spend your ride bouncing up and down like a motorboat on a high sea. This condition, in fact, is called "motor-boating," and is one of the indications that your shocks need some attention.

There's a test for shocks, too. With the car at rest, hop up on the front bumper and then hop off. Does the car oscillate up and down or does it come quickly back to the rest position? If it bounces, chances are that your shock absorbers need changing.

But the shocks do more than eliminate bouncing. By raising the car up on the springs, they provide a much smoother, softer ride. If

DAMPING
The purpose of damping is to reduce vibration by absorbing it in a spring. Instead of a manual spring, though, we have here a fluid spring: hydraulics.

Rubber bonded bush

Eye for attaching to car body

Piston rod

Working cyclinder

Control valve

Piston has tiny passage for fluid exchange

Recovery chamber

Rubber bush

Eye for attachment to axle or suspension link

TELESCOPIC DAMPER
When the wheel moves upwards, so does the cylinder. Oil beneath the piston is pushed through the valve into the above chamber. On the recovery, oil goes back through another valve in the piston

your shock absorbers are bad, nothing will restore that "new car feel" the way a new set of shocks will.

Shock absorbers themselves are inexpensive. You can buy them for as low as five dollars per set. However, we have noticed in recent years that many of the companies that sell shocks sell them at a price that also includes the installation. In case you want the experience, we'll outline the necessary steps to changing your own. But you may decide to pay to have somebody else do this work, too. It's hard, it's dirty, and not much fun.

What kind of shocks should you buy? We like to buy the best we can afford so that we won't have to replace them too soon. However, unless you like a hard, high-lift ride, don't go for the big jobs. Not unless you're planning to carry excess weight or haul heavy loads.

To change the shocks, after you purchase the new ones (to fit your model car), raise the front of the car. You'll see the old shocks mounted vertically and at an angle. The chances are that the holding nuts will be frozen in place, and you may need some penetrating oil, a strong wrench and a heavy maul to budge them. Removing the nuts is your first job.

Once the nuts are free, the shocks should come off with relative ease, but putting the new ones in place will require a bit of jockeying as they won't have the play and give of the old worn ones. By jockeying with an axle and bumper jack at the same time, and with a lot of effort, it is possible to mount the shocks and finally replace the nuts. But we prefer to relegate this task to an able mechanic.

There are no adjustments for shock absorbers. When you get the old ones off, you will notice that they slip up and down with little effort, while the new ones took some pressure to make them move.

Transmissions

There isn't much you can do with the car's transmission once it goes completely bad, except to take it to a transmission specialist. With sufficient time, the seals dry and go bad, and you start to lose transmission fluid. When this happens, you will feel the car "slip" as it goes through the gears, and when the transmission fluid level gets low enough, you can sit there and race your engine with the car in gear. You aren't going to go anyplace.

To check the level of fluid in the transmission, you must do it with the engine running, and preferably warmed up. You'll find a dipstick, looking somewhat like the oil dipstick, under the hood above the transmission. Insert the dipstick to its maximum depth, withdraw it, wipe it, and reinsert it. Withdraw it again and read the level. If fluid is needed, add additional fluid until the level of "full" on the dipstick is reached.

If the car is so old that you suspect dried-out seals, use a transmission fluid with a built-in

"seal treatment." Unfortunately, you won't get any other indication that your transmission fluid is low, except that sometimes subtle slippage, until you develop a problem. So always make it a point to check this when you get the chance and find yourself under the hood anyway.

Once you start adding transmission fluid, chances are you can get along pretty well by simply pouring a can of fluid into the transmission whenever it is needed. However, there is a law of diminishing returns, when adding fluid gets to be more expensive than a transmission job would be. When you start to feel the pinch in your budget, it's time to see a transmission mechanic.

Once you start to lose fluid, things can only get worse. You can save some costly tow-truck charges by getting it taken care of. Do not attempt to replace seals yourself. You might get it right, but a misplaced seal can result in trouble later.

Your transmission expert will also recommend what is called a transmission "tune-up." You can tune up an engine by setting the timing and the carburetor, but what, we wondered, was a transmission tune-up? One mechanic explained it this way: "The bands that make a transmission operate at all are inclined to stretch after much use. When we talk about tuning-up the transmission, what we do is tighten those bands so there's less slop, less play, and better action."

Fine. Just make sure that you know what you're going to be paying for when you approve work to be done.

The Clutch

Many of today's cars use automatic transmissions of one sort or another. However, there has been a recent trend back to the old days when cars had a clutch pedal to the left of the brake pedal, and a gear-shift stick emerging from the floor boards. Today's youngsters seem to think that there's glamor in racing an engine and manually shifting through gears. Your author learned to drive on what we called a "stick shift," which gives his own age away, but that same system is now called "four on the floor" and proves that you can sell anything if you rhyme it.

We once had a French import that used a "Ferlec" automatic clutch. When you moved the gear shift only slightly, the clutch would disengage the gearbox from the transmission, then re-engage it when the stick was released. We were having trouble with the fool thing, and complained about it at work one day. A young engineer who was born and raised in France, asked if he could look at it.

As we walked out to the company parking lot, he asked if I kept the car in a garage. I did, I told him. "Ah," he said. "Zat is zee troble. You are spoiling him!"

He instructed me to put the key in the ignition and turn it on, but not to start the engine. I did. He opened the hood, spotted the little black Ferlec box, and picked up a stick. To my horror and amazement, he proceeded to whale away at the box, screaming at it in French, using words

my French teacher in high school never taught me.

He finished up by dropping the stick and slamming the hood. "I weel teach you not to work!"

Okay. I know. He might have shook a relay loose. Maybe he separated a short. I don't know. All I know is that I never had any more trouble with the fool thing—except once when it bucked a bit and I opened the hood and screamed "I'll take you back to Pierre!"

What I'm trying to say is that when you're dealing with things automotive, you have to decide whether to take advantage of a cost opportunity or have a mechanic who knows do the work for you.

In this chapter, you have learned some of the basics of the more-difficult jobs in dealing with your car. Next, comes the car's electrical system—where things happen, and you are rarely able to see parts move.

6
The Electrical System

If there's any part of the car that must be called the "heart," it is the electrical system. This system provides for starting the car, operating the ignition, the horn, the head and tail lights, the heater fan, and the air conditioner. Your car's radio operates electrically, and on some cars, the windshield wipers and many other accessories operate electrically.

The basis of the electrical system is the car's storage battery. This is a wet cell type that uses chemical action to provide the electricity. The battery is connected through the voltage regulator to the car's alternator which generates twelve volts of electricity when the car's engine is operating. When the engine turns, the crankshaft operates the alternator through a belt system. The voltage generated by the alternator passes through the regulator to the battery. The regulator cuts off the alternator's action when the battery is fully charged. As you can see, operating the car will re-charge a low battery, keeping it in peak condition.

The battery connects through the starter switch to the starter motor, which is an electric motor, geared to the engine crankshaft. Closing the starter motor switch will therefore cause the engine to crank and the car to start.

The battery also provides voltage to the coil. This is a transformer that increases the twelve volts to a much higher voltage. This increased voltage is passed to the distributor, which feeds the higher voltage to the spark plugs in proper sequence, so the engine will fire. In addition to these engine-operating functions, the electrical system provides the many luxuries and necessities that your car depends on for sure, safe, comfortable operation.

Preventive Maintenance: The Battery

As with any other system in your car, the best kind of maintenance is preventive maintenance. You do the work *before* something goes bad, thereby avoiding emergencies and unexpected down time.

Preventive maintenance must begin with the battery. The battery contains an acid solution and no impurities must be allowed to enter the acid. The electrolyte (the liquid inside the battery) should also be kept at the proper level. This means that every time you look under the hood, you should take the

Stationary windings in which current is generated

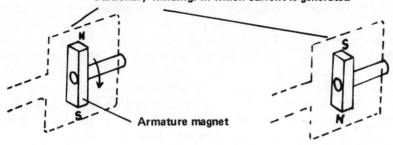

Armature magnet

Alternating current. As the armature, or rotor, turn the current is continually reversed.

THE ALTERNATOR

The turning magnet generates a current in the alternator's stationary winding

Terminals

In the solenoid switch a coil of many turns of wire encloses a soft iron plunger. When electricity —controlled by the driver's starter switch— flows through the coil, its magnetism moves the plunger, closing the contacts and allowing current to current to flow from the battery to the to the starter motor.

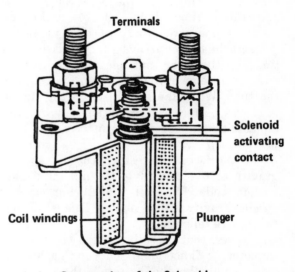

Solenoid activating contact

Coil windings

Plunger

THE SOLENOID SWITCH

Cross-section of the Solenoid showing coil windings, plunger and cable terminals

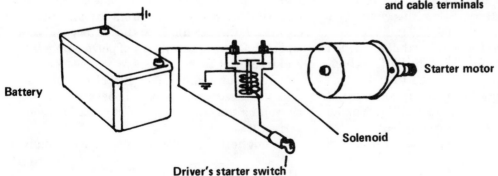

Starter motor

Battery

Solenoid

Driver's starter switch

time to remove the fill caps and check the level of the liquid. If any of the cells appear to be low, add water.

If you add ordinary tap water, however, you will also be adding impurities in the form of minerals and some chemicals that the water can contain. Although there are different schools of thought, at times outright controversy, regarding the use of tap water, I feel it's better to play it safe and use distilled water only. This is usually available at your local supply store, or, believe it or not, at your supermarket, where it is sold for filling steam irons. If you cannot obtain distilled water easily, get one of those charcoal filtering devices used for purifying tap water, and use that.

You should periodically check the rate of charge on your battery, too. This is a sure-fire indicator of impending battery failure, and will also indicate if your alternator is not functioning properly. You can do this with a specific gravity tester meant for the job. It consists of a glass tube, a rubber bulb at the top, and inside the glass tube, a weighted card called the float.

Insert the tube into the battery cells one at a time. By squeezing and releasing the rubber bulb, suck some of the fluid from the cell into the tube. When the float rises in the liquid, read the battery cell condition on its card. Squeeze the bulb again to squirt the fluid back into the cell.

The specific gravity tester checks the specific gravity of the electrolyte (liquid) inside the battery cells. If a cell is well-charged, the specific gravity will be higher. This is all that this device tells you.

However, that is really quite a bit. For the ammeter or "idiot lamp" on your dashboard tells you only that the "battery"—the combined total of the cells—is charging. The specific gravity tester can indicate that you've got a bad cell in the battery. Something your idiot light cannot do.

This reminds me of something that happened when I was working for one of the big "mechanical" magazines. An author had thought up a really unique device for a car. It consisted of three small bulbs that were mounted to a panel on the dash. These were connected to three small carbon rods that he got out of used "D"

cells. He enlarged the breather cap holes in the cell tops, and inserted a carbon rod until it touched the liquid level. Know what happened? The three lamps on the dash lit up brightly, indicating that all cells were fully charged, and that there was sufficient water in the cells. If the lights dimmed, it would indicate that the cell feeding the dim light wasn't putting out properly. If a light went out, the liquid level was low. Sounds like a great idea, doesn't it? But wait until you hear what happened.

When a battery operates, it gives off hydrogen gas. And hydrogen, as the people on the Hindenberg found out, is a volatile, explosive gas. Now when a circuit opens or closes, a spark can be generated. And when a battery is bouncing around in a car, the liquid sloshes, and . . . You guessed it! Anybody that tried to install this system in his own car, sooner or later blew his battery up!

But back to the specific gravity tester. It has a card inside it that is held in a small glass vial with some lead weights at the bottom. The card is colored red, yellow and green, to indicate whether the cell is charged, in trouble, or just plain bad.

You can also check cell condition by using an under-load battery voltmeter which imposes an artificial load on the cell while you read the voltage. An ordinary voltmeter won't suffice, for unless a cell is checked with a load, it will read satisfactory, even if it isn't! You can usually borrow such a meter from your local mechanic. He'll be happy to cooperate, for if you want to test your battery, he might get the idea that you're having troubles and may decide to buy a new one from him.

You may notice a collection of white residue around the anode of the battery. If you see this stuff, mix a solution of borax and water, use a stiff brush, and get rid of it. Now loosen and remove the battery cables from the terminals, clean both the terminals on the battery and the end of the cables, apply a bit of petroleum jelly, and reconnect them.

While you're going over the electrical system, make sure you check all operating lights, as well as the horn. If you find a malfunction, correct it.

Do not hesitate to inspect the cables. Simply

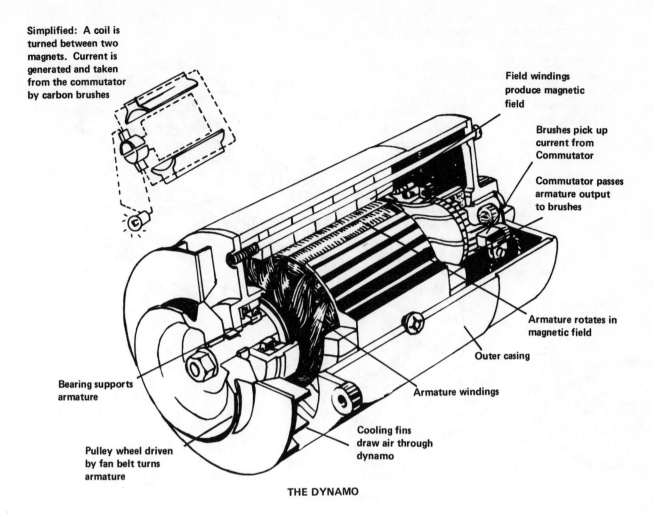

Simplified: A coil is turned between two magnets. Current is generated and taken from the commutator by carbon brushes

Field windings produce magnetic field

Brushes pick up current from Commutator

Commutator passes armature output to brushes

Armature rotates in magnetic field

Outer casing

Armature windings

Cooling fins draw air through dynamo

Bearing supports armature

Pulley wheel driven by fan belt turns armature

THE DYNAMO

follow each electrical cable and wire from point to point, making sure that all insulating material is intact. Check the terminal points of each wire, and use a screwdriver to make sure that the terminals are tight, where screw terminals are used. A cable whose insulation is falling away must be replaced or you run the risk of a serious under-hood fire.

Check the wires running from distributor to spark plugs and from coil to distributor. Remember, your car engine vibrates, and these can work loose.

The deadly enemies of your car's electrical system are oil and grease. Unfortunately, grease is exactly what you've got a lot of under the hood. This grease can settle on the surfaces of your wires, or you can accidentally spill some oil on a wire harness. If this happens, clean things up at once, using a non-petroleum type degreaser. In fact, because of the atmosphere in which these wires are located, it's a good idea to get the muck off the wires periodically anyway.

Remove the harness from the spark plugs, and remove the plugs if there is a collection of grease on the white porcelain insulator of the plugs. If sufficient grease does settle there, you may run into the possibility of a high-resistance short between the terminal and the threaded block. This can steal energy from a plug and result in a misfire.

When you replace the spark plug connector, make sure that it seats tightly and firmly and does not feel loose. If it does, remove it again,

STARTER MOTOR A toothed pinion moves along the rotating shaft of the motor, which is operated by current from the battery, to engage the teeth on the flywheel and turn it, starting the engine. It is often the spring which operates the return of the pinion which becomes jammed and must be cleaned or replaced.

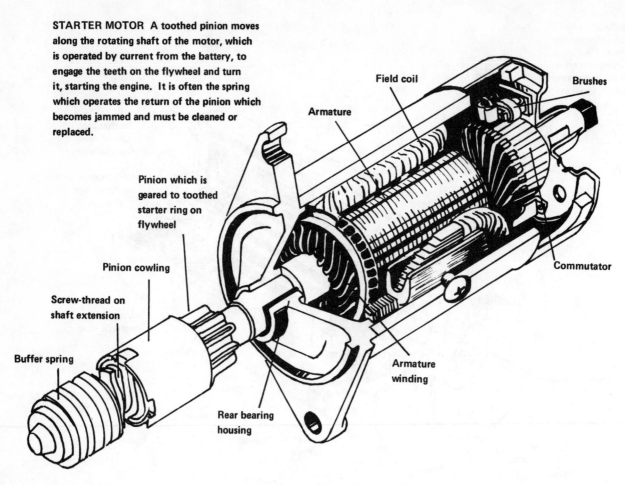

Field coil

Brushes

Armature

Pinion which is geared to toothed starter ring on flywheel

Pinion cowling

Screw-thread on shaft extension

Buffer spring

Commutator

Armature winding

Rear bearing housing

CROSS-SECTION OF A STARTER MOTOR

and using your fingers only, squeeze the connector cap to tighten the fit on the plug.

Corrective Maintenance

There are some things that can go wrong with your car's electrical system that you cannot correct by yourself. If your car's battery does not charge, it could be the generator or alternator, or perhaps the relay in the regulator is stuck in the wrong position. Before you can do much to rectify a problem such as this, you will want to get the car started so you can isolate the cause of the fault.

The first thing to do is get the battery recharged, but this is not always all that easy. If

you do not have a charger, you'll want to bring the battery to a local service station that does have a charger. If you aren't that far from the service station, you could borrow a battery-carrying strap from them, remove the battery and lug it over there for charging. Short of that, get hold of a good set of jumper cables, available at under two dollars from any auto supply shop. Pull another car up alongside yours, then raising both hoods, connect the jumper from the good battery to your dead one.

Observe proper polarity. If you bring your battery to a service station for charging, you need not be concerned about polarity, for the attendant will hook it up properly. If you have your own charger, the instructions that come with it will tell you how the battery to be charged should be connected. Generally, however, positive goes to positive, negative to negative. These terminals are usually marked + for positive, − for negative, or the terminals and lead wires can be color-coded, with red representing positive, black representing negative.

With the batteries properly hooked up, start the engine of the "rescue" car, and when it is running, attempt to start yours. The good battery will kick your engine over. Without turning your engine off, disconnect the cables and note on your ammeter whether or not your battery is charging. If it is not, the problem is in the ignition system of your car and you'll have to take it to your mechanic to handle.

Light Bulbs

Naturally, when a lamp burns out, you're going to change it. However, always take care to see that you put everything back in place the way it belongs. One chap who had occasion to change tail lamps must have been totally oblivious to the problem that his lamp-changing created. He did not take care to see that the rubber grommet between the tail-light lens and the chrome mounting ring was properly seated, and we became aware of the problem by following him along a dark road on a very rainy night. His tail-light assembly had almost filled with water which was sloshing about inside, and was already well over the level of the lamp!

As you may gather, water will do the electrical system no good at all. The owner of this car must remove the tail-lamp assembly, straighten or replace the grommet, and then reassemble it properly. What's more, he should thoroughly dry the area, for you can bet that the nice, shiny metal parts will rust and thereby reduce the reflection available from the chromed parts.

Whenever you have occasion to change a lamp such as this, do whatever maintenance you can while things are still apart. If you look into the lamp socket, for example, you'll see a small brass or copper contact that normally rests against the base of the lamp. While the

lamp is out, use an ordinary pencil eraser to reach into the socket and then rotate the eraser against the contact to clean any oxidation away. Oxidation can reduce or impede the progress of electricity to the lamp, and many a bulb that was thought to be burned out has simply gathered a collection of oxidation at its base.

One problem area that you can often service yourself without getting into trouble, is the distributor. Your local service shop can provide you with a kit of replacement parts for your distributor. This kit will contain a new condenser and a set of breaker points, along with full installation instructions.

Begin by prying away the two clamps that hold the distributor cap in place, and simply lift the cap aside. There is no need to remove the wires. Reach into the distributor and remove the rotor by simply lifting it away.

Now you will have access to the condenser, which is held in place by a single mounting screw. We prefer to use a grabber screwdriver for this, so we don't drop the screw. Loosen the screw to which the condenser lead goes, and slip the connector out from under the screw head.

Now put the lead of the new condenser under the screw, and tighten it down. Position the condenser inside the distributor body and replace the mounting screw.

You may notice, when you replace the breaker points, that they are gouged or pitted. If so, this replacement will indeed improve your spark and your performance, too.

The Car Radio

When you travel any appreciable distance at all, you become dependent on the car radio. As you are already aware, problems with the radio go above and beyond the abilities of even the best auto mechanic, and such ministrations fall under the purview of a specialist. Like all specialists, he's expensive.

However, we have some experience in radio repair, and could not justify to ourselves the excessively high cost of some of the repair jobs we've seen where, for example, only a small, inexpensive component had to be changed. So, seizing the initiative, we visited a radio service shop and confronting the owner, we asked him to explain his exorbitant prices. Defensively, he did so.

The biggest problem in most of these repairs is removing and reinstalling the radio chassis. It seems that some of the Detroit designers feel that the radio module will never need work, and they bury it up and under in such a way that, on some of those cars, the only way to get the radio out is to disassemble half the dashboard. It is this part of the work that occupies the greatest part of the cost, and while the actual work on the radio requires the services of a skilled technician, the removal and replacement uses his expensive time, and you foot the bill.

We solved this problem nicely, thank you.

When a radio goes sour, we pull it out ourselves. We took the chassis into the service shop in our own hands, and not only did we save a small fortune on the repair job, but the shop owner was eternally grateful, too. He got to charge more to take the set out, but he'd really rather charge less and avoid that work.

I know what you're thinking. If it's such a tough job, why should I do it myself? Mostly because you can; and if you don't, it will cost too much to have the man in the service shop do it.

Be warned, however. Maybe you've experienced one success after another in working on your car, but that radio must be declared out of bounds. Make no effort to repair the car radio unless you have a full knowledge of radio servicing. For one thing, chances are that if the set is still under warranty or guarantee, the manufacturer has protected himself with a small paper patch or a spot of colored enamel over one or more of the screws that hold the radio's cover plates in position. To remove the plate, you have to break the seal, and that also voids your warranty. Only an authorized serviceman may break these with impunity, and he has new ones to replace them with. Do not remove these yourself, nor allow any unauthorized people to do so, regardless of how competent you judge them to be.

Spark Plugs

Now let's talk about the spark plugs, which are also an important part of the car's electrical system.

There is one plug for each cylinder in the engine. A four-cylinder car will have four plugs, a six-cylinder engine has six. The spark is generated electrically. Battery voltage is fed to a transformer-like coil that boosts the voltage, and then this higher voltage goes to the distributor, a rotary device that is synchronized with the crankshaft of the engine. When a given piston is raised in the cylinder to compress the gases, at the apex of the rise, that spark plug will fire, igniting the gases and causing a small explosion inside the cylinder. Now let's see what that word "explosion" means. An explosion need *not* be destructive. It is a rapid burning of the gases. This drives the piston downward, the piston rod is connected to the crankshaft, and so the shaft rotates.

Back at the spark plug, the distance that the spark jumps—called the gap distance—is critical. Make it too close, and you won't get a good enough spark to ignite the gas. Make it too large, and there won't be sufficient power for the spark to be created at all.

Because the spark operates in a high compression, explosive atmosphere, it is subject to carbonizing, fouling and, of course, the natural wear and erosion that you might expect from any component that constantly has a live spark dancing around on its working surface.

To correct spark plug problems, we usually replace the relatively inexpensive plugs, but if there is sufficient terminal surface left, you need only clean the plugs, dress the tips with a file to make sure that they are smooth, and then reset the gap distance.

Let's follow a step-by-step procedure for installing a new set of spark plugs.

Start by purchasing everything that you are going to need, including a suitable set of spark plugs for the make, model and year of your car. If you do not have a spark-plug wrench, buy one of those, too. You will also require a suitable gapping tool.

Removing Spark Plugs

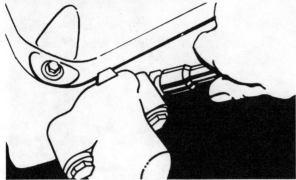

1 Gently rotate and pull boots and cable from the spark plugs.

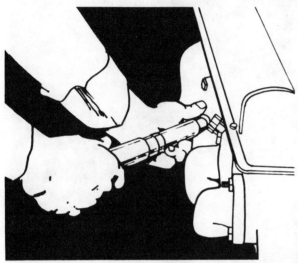

2 Loosen each plug but do not remove.

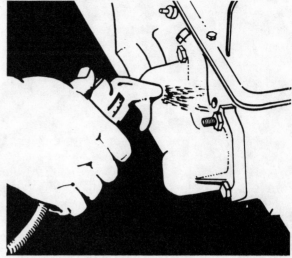

3 Air-blast dirt from the area around the plugs.

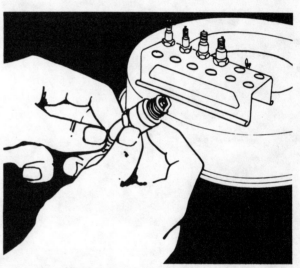

4 Remove each plug and place in a tray according to its position in the cylinder.

Begin the work by removing the old spark plugs one at a time. Be careful that nothing falls into the hole the spark plug was in, or whatever it is will wind up right inside the cylinder where it can only do damage.

Examine the plugs as you take them out. The tips should be dry, and not show any signs of wet oil, which would indicate the need for a ring job.

Set the old plugs aside, then using the gapping tool, set the space between the terminals to the specification designated for your own car.

Reinstall the new plugs, turning them in, finger tight. Using the spark-plug wrench (and a torque wrench if you have it), tighten the plugs to about 15 pounds of torque which will be sufficient for the plugs.

Before installing each new plug, make sure

Removed and held in the spark-plug wrench, this plug shows fouling deposit inside the tip.

that you have discarded the old plug washer and installed the new one that comes with the plug.

Earlier in this chapter, we mentioned cleaning the spark plugs. When you install a new set of plugs, it's a good idea to obtain a set of those soft rubber or plastic boots that are designed to slip over the body of the plug to protect it from dirt. These are inexpensive and are easy to install. They make a worthwhile investment.

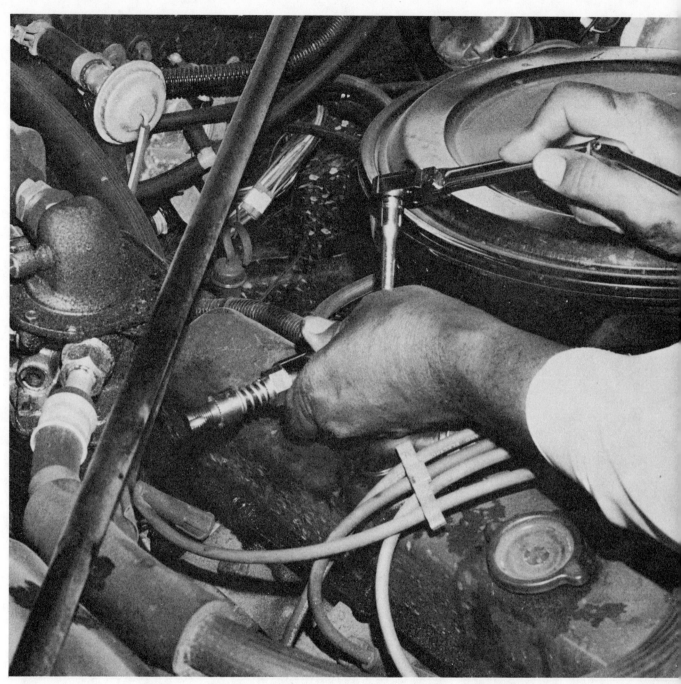

To clean spark-plug socket, attach thread chaser and seat cleaning tool to torque wrench.

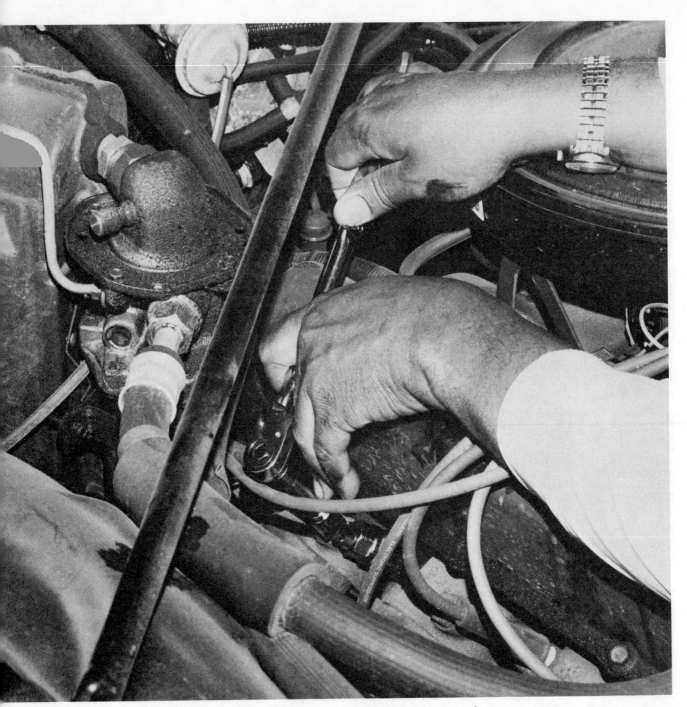

Place tool in spark-plug socket of cylinder head and rotate tool.

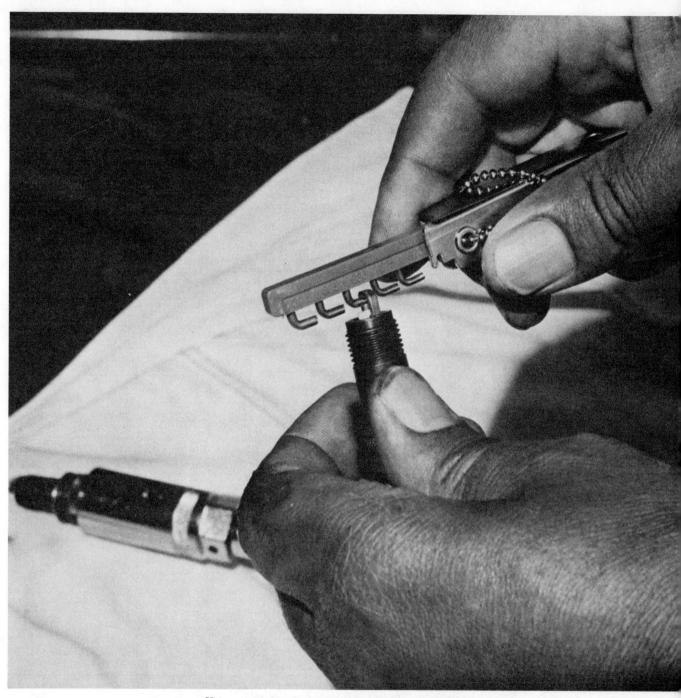

Using gapping tool, check spark-plug gap of replacement plug.

Set torque wrench to specified pounds-per-inch pressure for your plugs. Thread new spark plug "finger tight" using socket head.

Install replacement spark plug with wrench torquing as needed.

Cleaning and Adjusting Spark Plugs

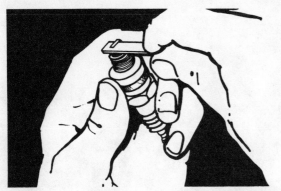

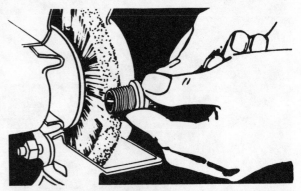

1 After surfaces are wiped clean and oily or wet firing-end deposits removed, clean electrodes with a gap gauge file.

2 A powered or hand wire brush is used to clean spark-plug threads of carbon and scale deposits.

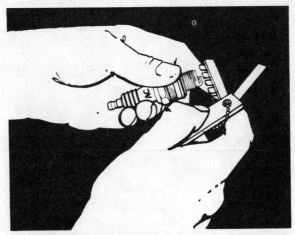

3 Use the proper tool to gap spark plugs . . . a spark-plug gap gauge.

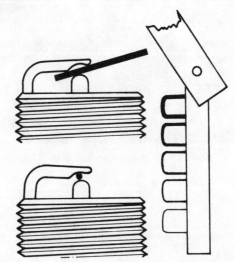

4 Always use a round wire gauge on used spark plugs, as a flat feeler gauge cannot accurately measure the gap of old plugs.

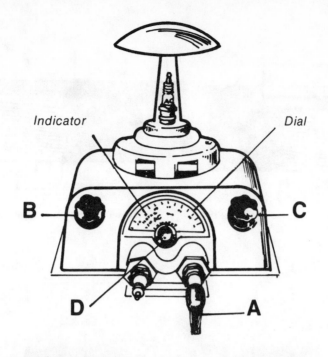

Indicator

Dial

B

C

D

A

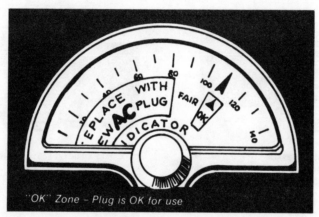

"OK" Zone – Plug is OK for use

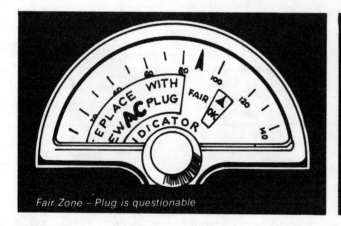

Fair Zone – Plug is questionable

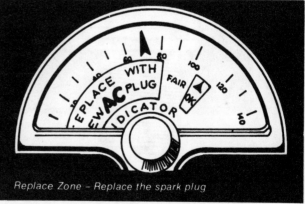

Replace Zone – Replace the spark plug

This model spark-plug cleaner and indicator compares worn plugs with a new plug of the correct type and indicates the need for replacement.

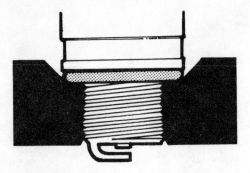

Spark plug with gasket correctly installed in cylinder head.

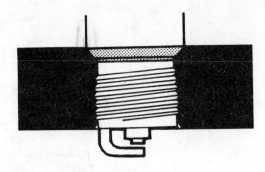

Taper seat spark plug correctly installed in cylinder head.

Installation Pitfalls to Avoid

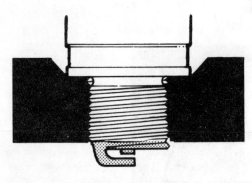

1 Spark plug installed without a gasket. This spark plug could overheat and cause pre-ignition. Threads projecting into the combustion chamber could clog with residue and make removal difficult.

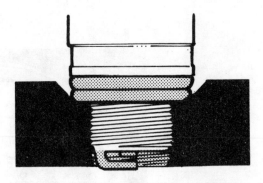

2 Spark plug installed with two gaskets. Exposed threads in the cylinder head can fill with residue making proper spark plug reinstallation difficult. Cylinder threads must be cleaned.

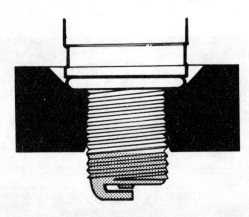

3 Long reach spark plug installed in cylinder designed for one with shorter reach. Pre-ignition could occur along with residue-filled threads which cause difficulties in spark-plug removal.

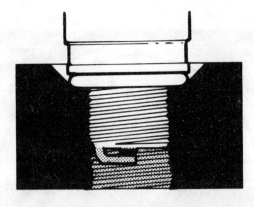

4 Spark plug with a short reach installed in cylinder head designed for a longer reach spark plug. Residue can fill cylinder threads . . . spark plug can easily foul and misfire. Reinstallation requires prior cleaning of cylinder threads.

Spark Plug Analysis Table

CONDITION	POSSIBLE CAUSE	CORRECTION
1. Carbon Fouling	Overrich carburetion, a sticking early fuel evaporation (EFE) valve, a faulty automatic choke, or a sticking manifold heat valve. A clogged air cleaner can restrict air flow to the carburetor causing rich mixtures. Poor ignition output (faulty breaker points, weak coil or condenser, worn ignition cables) can reduce voltage and cause misfiring. Excessive idling, slow speeds under light load also can keep spark plug temperatures so low that normal combustion deposits are not burned off.	After the cause has been eliminated, spark plugs may be cleaned, re-gapped and reinstalled. If carbon deposits are not burned off, a hotter AC Spark Plug will better resist carbon deposits.
2. Oil Fouling	May be caused by oil pumping past worn rings. "Break-in" of a new or recently over-hauled engine before rings are fully seated may also result in this condition.	Usually, these spark plugs can be degreased, cleaned and reinstalled. While hotter type spark plugs will reduce oil deposits, an engine overhaul may be necessary in severe cases to obtain satisfactory service.
3. Deposit Fouling "A"	Deposits which accumulate on the insulator are by-products of combustion and come from the fuel and lubricating oil, both of which today generally contain additives. Most powdery deposits have no adverse effect on spark plug operation; however, they may cause intermittent missing under severe operating conditions, especially at high speeds and heavy load.	If the insulator is not too heavily coated, the spark plugs may be cleaned, regapped and reinstalled.
4. Deposit Fouling "B"	Deposits are similar to those identified as "Deposit Fouling-A". These deposits are by-products of combustion and come from the fuel and lubricating oil. Excessive valve stem clearances and/or defective intake valve seals will allow excessive lube oil to enter the combustion chamber with the fuel. The deposits will accumulate on the portion of the spark plug projecting into the chamber and will be heaviest on the side facing the intake valve. Defective seals should be suspected when the condition is found in only one or two cylinders.	After the cause has been eliminated, the spark plugs may be cleaned, regapped and reinstalled.

Spark Plug Analysis Table (cont'd.)

CONDITION	POSSIBLE CAUSE	CORRECTION
5. Deposit Fouling "C"	Most powdery deposits, as shown in "A" have no adverse effect on the operation of the spark plug as long as they remain in the powdery state. However, under certain conditions of operation, these deposits melt and form a shiny glaze coating on the insulator which, when hot, acts as a good electrical conductor. This allows the current to follow the deposits instead of jumping the gap, thus shorting out the spark plug.	Glazed deposits can be avoided by not applying sudden load, such as wide open throttle acceleration, after sustained periods of low speed and idle operation. Glazed spark plugs must be replaced.
6. Detonation	Overadvanced ignition timing, or the use of low octane fuel will result in detonation, commonly referred to as engine knock or "ping." This causes severe shock inside the combustion chamber, resulting in damage to the adjacent parts which include spark plugs. A common result of prolonged detonation is to have the sidewire of a spark plug torn off.	After the cause has been eliminated, replace damaged plugs.
7. Preignition	Preignition indicates excessive overheating. Cooling system stoppage, sticking valves, or overlean air-fuel mixtures are common causes of preignition. Spark plugs which are the wrong (too hot) heat range, or not properly installed are also a possible cause. Sustained high speed, heavy load service can produce high temperatures which will cause preignition.	After the cause has been eliminated, replace damaged plugs with new AC Spark Plugs. For sustained high speeds or heavy loads install colder spark plugs.
8. Heat Shock Failure	Overadvanced ignition timing and low grade fuel are usually responsible for heat shock failures. Rapid increase in tip temperature under severe operating conditions causes the heat shock and a fracture results. Another common cause of chipped or broken insulator tips is carelessness in regapping by either bending the centerwire to adjust the gap, or allowing the gapping tool to exert pressure against the tip of the center electrode or insulator when bending side electrode to adjust the gap.	After the cause has been eliminated, replace damaged plugs.

Spark Plug Analysis Table (cont'd.)

CONDITION	POSSIBLE CAUSE	CORRECTION
9. Insufficient Installation Torque	Poor contact between the spark plug and the engine seat. The lack of proper heat transfer, resulting from poor seat contact, causes excessive overheating of the spark plug and, in many cases, severe damage as shown. Dirty threads in an engine head can also result in the plug seizing before it is seated.	Replace damaged spark plugs with new AC Spark Plugs. Observe torque specifications.
10. Proper Gasket Compression (For Applications Requiring a Gasket Seat Spark Plug)	Gasket compression shown in the tab photo was achieved by installing a new spark plug at 25 pound feet in clean threads. This gasket has conformed to the plug and engine seat to allow maximum heat transfer from plug to engine and to form a gas tight seal. (A properly compressed 14MM gasket will be .045" to .050" thick. A new gasket is .070" to .080".)	No correction required.
11. No Gasket Compression (For Applications Requiring a Gasket Seat Spark Plug)	Little or no force has been applied to the gasket. In actual installation, it is necessary to almost completely compress the gasket to allow proper heat transfer to the engine block.	Observe proper torque specifications.
12. Thread Seizure	Scaled and deposit filled threads have not allowed proper gasket compression (or seating). CAUTION: Proper installation torque may be attained without compressing the engine seat gasket for applications requiring a gasket seat spark plug. For taper seat applications, proper installation torque may be obtained without taper seat engagement in cylinder head. Operation of an engine with this type of installation can result in plug overheating and destruction of either the spark plug or engine, or both.	Insure cylinder head and spark plug threads are free of deposits, burrs and scales. Replace damaged plugs.

Spark Plug Analysis Table (cont'd.)

CONDITION	POSSIBLE CAUSE	CORRECTION
13. Manganese Deposits	Manganese additive in some fuels. These deposits of manganese dioxide (MnO_2) do not adversely affect operation of the spark plugs.	Spark plugs may be cleaned, re-gapped and reinstalled.
14. Improper Cleaning	Overblasting and not rocking spark plugs during cleaning results in dirty, damaged insulator tips. Eroded tips change heat range and conductive paths mean fouled spark plugs, both resulting in poor engine operation.	Replace improperly cleaned spark plugs.
15. Proper Cleaning		Follow recommended cleaning procedure of short abrasive blasts accompanied by rocking of the spark plug in the adapter, results in a properly cleaned spark plug ready to give many additional miles of service.
Normal Operation	Brown to grayish-tan deposits and slight electrode wear indicate correct spark plug heat range and mixed periods of high and low speed driving.	Spark plugs may be cleaned, re-gapped and reinstalled. When re-installing spark plugs that have been cleaned and regapped, be sure to use a new engine seat gasket in each case where gasket is required.

Accessories

You will be wooed by the various manufacturers with all sort of devices for which they make the wildest-sounding claims. Some of them are truly worthless, while others are so beneficial that the Detroit engineers have incorporated them into the newer models.

One recent innovation is the capacitive discharge ignition system. If your car isn't equipped with one, you can buy it as an accessory and install it yourself. Once installed, it will give you faster, easier starts, less spark plug wear, and no need to replace the points, as there *are* no points. It's an electronic, transistorized device and it does one heck of a good job. You can even leave your old system in place, just in case the CD system should fail, and you've got a redundant back-up as an added safety factor.

You'll find other, less expensive devices, designed to give you a "hotter spark." I don't know why, if your car is operating, that you'd want a hotter spark, but they sell a lot of these anyway. These things, encapsulated in bright red plastic as a rule, are designed to be installed between the coil and the distributor. Frankly, the coil is supposed to provide a hot enough spark, and if it is doing its job, you won't need any accessories of this sort.

We have also come across a series of assorted liquids and powders that are supposed to "help" the battery. The claims are usually implied rather than specified. One shows a mechanic—I guess he's a mechanic from the way he's dressed—holding a packet of the powder over a car's battery, saying "Your car never worked so good!" Frankly, there's nothing other than electrolyte that should be added to the battery, and that, only in the form of distilled water.

While we are talking about accessories, many years ago the Detroit manufacturers did away with the gauges and meters that told you about your car's operating condition. They replaced these with the so-called "idiot lights" that only light up to inform you of a problem. Now, many drivers are not content to know that their car's motor is overheated—they'd rather know that it is starting to overheat.

They don't want to know only that they have no oil pressure, they want to know how much oil pressure they have.

You can purchase such meters and gauges, nicely mounted in under-dash panels, and even equipped with small lamps that will light when you turn the car's headlights on. They offer a constant monitor for the car's system. They come in assorted sizes, prices and styles, and are easy to mount and connect. We consider these a worthwhile investment indeed.

You may question our reasoning here. "If these are so good, why didn't Detroit put them into the cars the way they once did?"

The big reason, of course, is design. The engineers simply felt that the recessed idiot lights looked better than the gauges and would be preferred by drivers. But, Detroit does not always know best.

Fuses

When you have as complicated an electrical system as you have in a car, you're going to require fuses to protect the several system components. You'll usually find the fuse block up under the dash of your car, usually mounted on the car's firewall. The fuse block may be protected by a plastic or metal cover.

What is a fuse? A fuse is a part of the electrical circuit, and electricity does flow through it. But the fuse consists of a soft metal, protected by glass and held by two end caps of a conducting material. Should a heavy surge of current occur, as will happen when something is wrong electrically, the heat of this current will cause the soft metal wire to melt, thereby opening the circuit. Fuses, by blowing out in this fashion, can prevent fires, and they can often stop a part from working just in time to prevent really serious damage to that part. However, you should understand that fuses don't get "weak" or "wear out." They are either good or they are bad.

If a fuse burns out, it will have to be replaced. But wait! What *made* the fuse burn out in the first place? If an electrical component went sour, and caused the fuse to blow out, replacing with a new fuse isn't going to help a thing, for the bad component will simply blow the new fuse, too! Before replacing the burned-out fuse with a new one, find out why the fuse burned out, get that fixed, and *then* replace the fuse.

Generally, you can locate a bad part with a simple circuit tester. Place one terminal of the tester to the chassis ground of the car, by clipping the lead either to the grounded pole of the battery or to the engine block itself. Touch the "hot" lead to the "hot" terminal of the suspect component. (Make sure the battery is not connected to the circuit. You can disconnect the battery by simply removing the hot wire.) If the meter indicates that there is direct continuity, the component is "shorted" and needs replacing.

As an easier test, consider that fuses are relatively inexpensive, and you can use a good fuse as a test. Disconnect all of the suspect components from the electrical circuit, and replace the fuse. It should *not* blow out. Now, proceed to connect the electrical components back into the circuit one at a time, checking the fuse as each component is added. When the fuse blows out, you've found your problem.

How can you tell if a fuse is good?

Some fuses, especially those that are rated at heavier amperages, will leave no question that they have burned out. The glass becomes black and murky, thanks to the spattering of the wire, and the wire itself will be seen not to be continuous.

However, the fuses rated for lighter currents consist of a hair-like wire that is difficult to see. These require a continuity tester. Use an ordinary flashlight bulb and battery. Make the fuse a part of your test circuit, and if the fuse is good, the lamp will light.

To make a fuse tester, take a flashlight and remove the bulb. Next, get a burned-out flashlight bulb and break the glass away. Connect two pieces of flexible, stranded wire to the two terminals in the bulb, by soldering them. Insulate the connections with tape, then put the *broken* bulb into the flashlight. Connect one of the wires to a small clip, such as an alligator clip, the other to the base of the good bulb. Connect the side terminal of the good bulb to another clip. To test a fuse, just place it between the clips and turn on the flashlight switch. If the bulb lights, the fuse is good.

There is a plastic tool called a fuse puller which will make checking and changing fuses a lot easier. While we have seen people change fuses using only a screwdriver for leverage, the screwdriver blade can cause shorts, make good fuses blow, and you usually wind up dropping fuses.

In this chapter, we've talked about your car's electrical system. We've discussed several of the things that can go wrong, and shown you how to rectify them.

In the next chapter, we're going to talk about the car's cooling system. You will learn that this not only can be kept from icing up in the winter, but from boiling over in the summer.

7
The Cooling System

We've already discussed the business of the "explosion" that occurs in each cylinder which, contrary to the bad connotation, is simply a rapid burning of gases under controlled conditions.

Of course, whether you call it burning or explosion, heat is a by-product. With heat, metals expand, and because the tolerances between cylinder wall and piston must be extremely close to keep the gases in the fire chamber, uncontrolled expansion can mean trouble. To help control the heat, we circulate water around the engine jacket at all times. Naturally, the water will heat up, too. We help dissipate this heat by circulating the water through the radiator, which is placed in front of the engine. We use a large fan to help cool the water. The car's water pump circulates the water through the entire system.

It's not all that simple, though.

Anti-freeze

The water passes through rubber tubes, metal components and, in some cases, various filtering devices. The water may contain impurities, which, acted upon by heat and circulation, can cause scale to form on the engine wall. Rusting is also a problem. We want to take as good care of the coolant as we can. To keep the water from boiling away when it reaches a temperature of 212° F. (the boiling point of water), we use certain additives. Typical of these is glycerine-based anti-freeze. Now wait. We said we wanted to keep the water from boiling away, so what are we doing with anti-freeze? Anti-freeze will indeed protect the water from freezing, but it has a most salutory effect in the summer, too. It keeps the water from boiling.

If you're smart, you're going to completely drain and flush your radiator before adding coolant anti-freeze. Now, to start with, you can run your car very nicely on anti-freeze alone, but this can be horrendously expensive. So what we usually do is use water as a coolant, and add anti-freeze to that.

How much anti-freeze?

The can of anti-freeze you buy will tell you how much protection you will have when you add the anti-freeze. If you want protection to a certain number of degrees, add the specified amount of anti-freeze.

Or, you can check the temperature to which your coolant is protected against freezing with a specific gravity tester, similar to the one used to check your car battery, which you can borrow or purchase for well under five dollars.

Naturally, the water *is* going to heat up, and we use this heat by pumping the heated water through the car's heater. The hot water heater has a fan that blows across a smaller version of the car's radiator, and expels the heated air into the car to provide additional comfort on a cold day. That's why your car's heater will provide no heat at all until the water has warmed up!

To accelerate this heating process in the winter, a thermostat is installed in the water line at the top of the engine block. The thermostat is a heat-controlled valve that remains closed until the engine water has reached a pre-set temperature, which allows the valve to open, permitting cold water to circulate in the block. This permits the water in the engine's jacket to heat up a good deal faster than it could if a constant supply of cool water was allowed to circulate.

What Can Go Wrong?

Usually, when you develop coolant troubles, your car's overheat lamp will light. This indicates that trouble exists, and the number of things that can go wrong are manifold—in fact, the manifold can be the root of one of the problems!

One of the basic problems can be with the thermostat, which can stick in either the open or closed position. You will observe a large hose that connects the radiator to the engine block. If you loosen the four bolts that hold this hose to the block, and remove the hose, you will see the thermostat sitting in its recess at the top of the engine. Removal is simply a matter of lifting the old thermostat out. You can replace this with a new thermostat simply by putting the new one in place—just make sure that you've got the right side pointing down! When you buy a new thermostat, there will be a new gasket, preformed and punched to fit in place.

Remove the old gasket, cleaning away any and all parts of it that may remain in place, and then put the new gasket and thermostat in position, replace the hose and the holding bracket, re-attach the bolts, and tighten them down. The job is done.

While you've got that hose disconnected, take a look at its insides. If you see any signs of brittleness, sponginess, softness, cracking or dryness, you may decide that this is a good time to replace the hose with a new one. While you are at it, if one hose is showing signs of wear, chances are that the others are too, and you'll want to replace all of them. Generally, in a car, there are four lengths of hose with which you will be concerned. These are: The hose that leads from the top of the radiator to the engine block, the hose that leads from the engine block to the radiator at the bottom, and the inlet and outlet hoses for the car's heater. In many automobiles, the radiator hoses are preformed and shaped, and can be obtained in the correct size and configuration at your local suppliers. The heater hoses are usually high-pressure hoses that you simply order in the correct diameter and length. While the hoses are removed, examine the hose clamps that are used to hold them in place, and replace these if you see any signs of rust, pitting, or wear. Always make sure that your new hoses follow the paths that the old hoses took, so they will be *away* from heat that may scorch the rubber, or away from moving components that can cut or abrade.

The coolant itself can be saved and reused from year to year, with perhaps an additional bit of coolant being added. However, the rust inhibitor in the coolant must be replaced each year. You can, if you desire, use the coolant again, but if you elect to do this, always throw a can of rust inhibitor into the system to refresh it and protect the "innards" of the cooling system.

Once in awhile, perhaps every two or three years or so, you're going to want to drain and cool the system.

Remove the radiator cap, and reach down to the petcock, a small valve near the base of the radiator. Open this, and the water will drain from the radiator. Allow it to remain open until water stops coming out, which indicates that the radiator is empty. Close the petcock and refill the radiator with a garden hose. Replace the radiator cap and start the engine allowing it to run until it is heated up and the thermostat has opened. Turn on the car's heater and allow this to run for awhile to allow the water to circulate through that, too.

Now repeat the process. With the engine off, open the petcock and drain the water, close the petcock, refill the radiator, and start the engine.

During this process, you might want to use a radiator-flush chemical, which will accelerate the cleaning and do a better job for you. Make certain the flush chemicals are drained away before you consider the job completed.

Now close the petcock and put about a quart of water in the radiator, then add the amount of coolant you wish to install. Fill the radiator the rest of the way, stopping well before the fill mark and overflow tube. Start the engine and allow the coolant to circulate fully after the thermostat has reached operating temperature. After this, the coolant level will decrease somewhat, and you can add a sufficient amount of water to bring the level almost to the fill mark.

That Radiator

Your radiator consists of copper tubing that is bent in a zig-zag pattern and fitted with cooling vanes or fins. Because the newer cars have pressurized water systems, you may find that a pin-hole leak can spurt coolant from the radiator. If you find that you are losing water, do not panic. The cure need not be horrendously expensive as in the old days, when the only cure was to remove the radiator, find the leak, and solder it up. Today, we have chemicals that will seal small leaks, and indeed, many manufacturers of anti-freeze add such chemicals to the anti-freeze. You gain the benefit of it, whether you need it or not. If your coolant additive doesn't have this chemical, you can buy it at your local supply store and add it yourself.

If it works, pat yourself on the back, and count the money you've just saved. If it doesn't

work, the only remaining cure is to visit your local mechanic and see what curative steps he advises.

What makes the water circulate through the entire system instead of just remaining in one place is a device called the water pump. This is usually located at the front of the engine block, and is connected to the crankshaft by means of a belt-and-pulley arrangement.

There's not much in the way of preventive maintenance that you can apply to the water pump, but you ought to know that it usually has friction problems of its own. You should locate this part on your own car, check to see if it has a grease fitting of its own, and make certain that each time the mechanic greases your car, the water pump fitting gets a shot, too.

You should also know that the water pump will usually fail while the car is being used. It's rare indeed for this component to stop operating while the car is at rest, and this means that you'll be on the road when trouble develops. What generally happens is that the water in the cooling system will exit in a rush, and your overheat lamp will come on shortly thereafter.

Try *not* to drive without coolant in the car. However, in an emergency, you can manage by periodically shifting the car to neutral, and accelerating the engine, which will allow the fan to do a better job of cooling. You will save your car, however, by waiting at the roadside for help.

Hoses

If you're caught in a sudden freeze without sufficient anti-freeze, chances are that the water in the lines will freeze, blocking them so water cannot flow. The pressurized system builds up (there's no place for the water to go) and a hose may burst, spilling your coolant all over the road. If this happens, pull up to the side of the road and, if you can, locate a replacement hose. This might not be easy to do.

We mentioned earlier that we once drove an imported French automobile. The little tag inside the engine compartment read *"Avec antigel. Protection – 32°."* That, clearly translated by my wife who spoke French, meant "With anti-freeze. Protected to minus thirty-two degrees." What she didn't think of telling me, however, was that the French used the Centigrade system, and my protection was nowhere near what I thought it was! On the road, one cold day, I had a freeze-up, and the loud bang from under the hood indicated trouble. Opening the hood revealed a gash in the hose—and, naturally, there was not a service station in sight. But, even if there were, there was little chance they'd have the right hose, anyway.

The tool kit in our trunk offered a possible solution, however. We carefully wrapped the hose with rubber tape, overlapping every half turn. We went back over this again, to put a double layer in place.

By this time, the engine heat of the standing car had melted the ice blockage in the lines, and the remaining small amount of water was sufficient to get us to a local gas station, where we filled up with additional water. We left the radiator cap off, too, to keep pressure from straining the tape unnecessarily.

The next day we got the hose replaced, and offered a few bitter words to the French mechanic who tried to explain the difference between Centigrade and Farenheit. We added some additional "antigel" and were on our way, sadder but wiser.

In this chapter, we've given you some background on your car's cooling system and some of the ills it might be heir to.

In the next chapter, we'll talk about lubricants and lubrication. You'll learn to catch the parts that mechanics always seem to miss.

8
Lubricating Your Car

Whenever a metal part rubs on metal, wear will take place. To reduce the wear factor (you really can't eliminate it) we use lubricants. Where the friction is relatively light, we use oil. Where more friction is encountered, we use heavier greases.

Unfortunately, these lubricants rarely last for too long a time. They can be squeezed out of where they are needed or, under the pressure of heavy friction and wear, they can be broken down and will no longer serve their function. If water enters the places where they are required, and pressure is added, the lubricants can combine with the water and emulsify.

The best solution to the lubricant problem is to replace the lubricant as often as replacement is needed.

To further complicate the problem, after oil has been used in the car's engine for awhile, it will pick up metal flakes and wear, and will become more of an abrasive than a lubricant.

Time For an Oil Change

Can you change your own oil? Sure you can. But you'll need an oil-change kit, and your local service shop can provide you with this. You'll also want a new oil filter, so get one at the same time.

To begin the process, use a web wrench to remove the old oil filter. In the oil-change kit, you'll find a large plastic bag that is fitted with a threaded tube that attaches where the oil filter was. Screw it firmly into place. Now start the engine, and you will observe that the engine oil, normally passed to the filter, fills the plastic bag instead. When the bag is full, the engine will have been drained of oil, and you didn't spill a drop on the floor of your garage! Carefully unscrew the plastic bag full of oil, replace the cap, and dispose of the oil-filled bag in the garbage.

Now put the new oil filter in place, tightening it down with the web wrench, once you have the threads properly engaged.

Remove the oil filler cap, and add the new oil, until you have put the correct amount into place. You have completed an oil change, and all it cost you was the price of the oil-change kit, the new oil, and a new filter, both of which you would have had to pay the mechanic for anyway!

Greasing the Car

Can you also grease your car? Indeed you can. But before you attempt this task, make sure that you know where all the grease fittings are located. Arm yourself with a pressure-type grease gun, filled with the recommended grade of grease. Have a clean rag along with you to clean the fittings of road dirt and impacted grease.

Jack the car so you can have access to its bottom, and wipe each grease fitting clean. With one hand, apply the grease gun to the fitting, and with the other hand, squeeze the trigger to expel grease from the gun. The grease will be forced into the fitting and into place, where it can do the most good. Continue to fill the fitting until you see clean grease emerging from the joint.

If you do not miss any of the fittings, you can in this way grease your own car, and save the cost that the mechanic would charge.

Spraying

While spraying was once a standard part of any chassis lubrication, it is rarely done by mechanics anymore. The reason for this is obscure, but if you do the work yourself, there is no reason why you can't spray. Get a good grade of universal oil in an aerosol can, and simply spray all parts of the under-chassis area.

This will provide lubrication for those component parts that ordinarily are overlooked. While spraying is not the best way to reach these parts, putting *some* lubricant into them is better than overlooking them entirely.

Other Areas

Remembering that lubrication is supposed to reduce wear on moving parts, you will want to add lubricant to such things as door hinges and locks. Some of these are fairly easy to lubricate, others are less accessible.

The door hinges should be given a healthy application of a good white grease. Operate the door while you are putting the grease in place, and by all means, *do* use too much! Moving the door back and forth will work the grease into place (or out of place, but at least it will be working the grease and showing you where you might have missed) and assure smoother door operation. Don't just do the hinges or mounts, either. Get the locks and latches, too. The door's hold-open device should also be greased.

On most cars, the latch consists of a star-shaped device that rotates with each slam of the door. This means that you will have to apply grease to each segment of the star, closing the door to rotate it each time.

The car's door handles should be lubricated, too, but apply this lubricant sparingly. Use a rag, too, in case any of the oil drips down on the car's finish. Oil can damage the finish if it is allowed to simply sit on the paint.

Open both the hood and the trunk lid, and apply grease to the working parts of both. In the trunk lid area, you will want some grease on the hinges as well as on the latch. Under the hood, you will have a complex latching mechanism that you will want to lubricate, and don't forget the hinge and the springs which serve as counterweights to make the hood easier to lift.

The various locks on the doors and trunk lid call for some special treatment, too. You should not use an oil-type lubricant on these, as this might cause the tumblers and pins to freeze up or bind when the oil becomes sludgy.

Instead, we use a dry powdered graphite. You can obtain this special lubricant in a small vial, with a narrow spout.

To use the graphite, remove the cover tip from the spout, and make a small hole in the spout with a sharp razor blade. Insert this into the keyway and squeeze the vial to blow the graphite into place. Remove the spout, and insert the operating key. Push it in and out of the lock several times, to work the graphite into place.

Having done this, apply additional graphite, and then insert the key and rotate it so that all internal parts of the lock are coated with graphite. Do this several times, to make sure the lock will operate properly. Wipe away any excess at once.

Lubricating Additives

Because of the very nature of a car, there are certain places that you will be unable to get at to lubricate.

However, it's a good idea to use a lubricating oil additive once in awhile, as follows. When you change oil, add one can of this additive to the car's crankcase. The top of the can will lift off, you open the oil filler cap while the engine is running at temperature, and slowly pour the heavy, viscose additive into the oil.

When your oil level is down sufficiently to add another quart of oil, add another can of the additive as well.

Approximately every thousand miles, pour a can of the gasoline additive into the gas tank. This will provide a measure of lubrication to those parts that the gasoline reaches. These super-lubricators will provide additional miles of trouble-free performance for your car.

What *Not* to Lubricate

Lubricants, those oils and greases that do such wonderful things for the metal parts, are a threat to rubber and many plastics. Being petroleum derivatives, they can wreak havoc to rubber and those plastics which have the same petroleum base. When you allow oil to touch rubber, the rubber softens, weakens, and will ultimately give way.

You will also come upon certain "permanently lubricated" bearings. These are of a special phosphor bronze material that has oil impregnated throughout its construction. Theoretically, the oil that is in the material will provide the necessary lubrication through the life of the part. You should refer to the manual for your car and act accordingly.

Many of the parts in a car are treated with a special Teflon material to help reduce friction. These parts will be indicated in your owner's manual as not requiring further lubrication. As some oils and solvents can attack the Teflon, avoid the application of oil to such components.

In the early days of machine design, a natural wood called *Lignum Vitae* was used in bearings and gears. This hard wood gave off a grease-like substance that provided permanent lubrication for the part. Naturally, no wooden parts are used in a car today save for decorative purposes or, in the case of one British-made automobile, for use in the chassis. This brings up another interesting anecdote.

When Henry Ford designed the first of his automobiles, he was very particular about how certain parts were to be shipped, specifying, for example, that the packing case shall be made of hardwood, with cross members placed thus and so, and with reenforcement as follows.

His packing designers could not understand why there was so much emphasis on the packing crates, which were normally disposed of. Ford, however, was adamant. If the people who sold parts to his firm wanted to continue to sell parts, they would provide the packaging as specified. They did.

When the first boxes arrived, the factory people began to tear the boxes open to get at the contents.

"Stop that!" Ford screamed.

He took the crowbar and proceeded to show the unpackers how to open the boxes. The entire top of the box had to be lifted off in one piece, and set aside.

"Why, Mr. Ford?" asked one of them. "We throw that stuff away!"

"Not any more, you don't. That top is going to be the floorboards of our new model!"

Conclusion

If you lubricate your car yourself, and to a great extent, you can, you will save two ways.

You will save quite a bit over the cost of a mechanic's service, and you will greatly extend the useful life of your automobile.

While a car may not need to have its oil changed precisely every 1,000 miles, it certainly pays to keep the various bearings well greased, and a good grade of oil in the crankcase—*clean* oil.

The only way to make sure that your oil is clean is to drain the old, used oil periodically and replace it. Your oil filter does a magnificent job, but from the time you install a new oil filter, it gets progressively less able to do its job. It requires replacing now and again, too.

9
The Engine

If there's one part of the car that's considered to be a "no man's land," it's the engine. Usually, people are right in not tampering with the engine, for in doing so, you can often do more harm than good. However, there *are* certain things you can do to improve the overall performance, and do so with no fear of causing irreparable damage.

Filters

There are usually several filters that you can be concerned with. In most cases, the filters clean dirt from the material that passes through them, and in doing so, they become dirty and clogged themselves. In time, when the filter has done its work for a sufficient period of time, either the trapped goo in the filter will pass through so the filter does not do its job any longer, or the filter becomes clogged so that the material to be passed through it can no longer pass. When this happens, the filter becomes a block.

In either case, the used filter must either be cleaned or replaced.

The *air filter* needs periodic attention. On top of the carburetor, you will find the air filter assembly. The cap is held in place by a wing nut that you can remove with your fingers. Lift the cover away, and you will see the air filter sitting in the breather.

To inspect the filter, simply remove it, and holding it against a strong light source, such as a bright sun, look through it. If you can see through the filter, it is clean and needs no further attention. If you cannot see through it, it must either be cleaned or replaced. Which you do is a function of the type of filter element that you have.

If the filter is of the plastic foam type, it can be cleaned by immersion and wringing in a small container of cleaning fluid, then allowed to dry, after which it can be replaced. If it is not cleanable, you must buy the correct filter replacement element, install it, and reassemble the cap and wing nut.

Oil filters these days are self-contained quart-size cans fitted with a threaded top that screws into the engine block. The old oil filter can be removed easily with a web wrench, and the new filter can be screwed in its place. Be careful when removing the old filter, as it will be full of dirty oil and is likely to drip.

The oil filter is usually changed when the oil is.

The fuel filter will be located somewhere in the fuel line between the fuel tank and the fuel pump or carburetor. On older cars, the fuel filter consisted of a small glass bowl with a ceramic element inside it. You could, if you kept the bowl clean, actually see foreign matter or water collecting at the bottom of the bowl, and cleaning the filter simply consisted of removing the bowl, emptying it, and then replacing it.

Modern cars use a sealed fuel filter unit that must be removed by taking off the intake and outlet nuts. The new filters cannot be cleaned, and must be replaced.

The PCV Valve

The crankcase gets its ventilation via the *Positive Crankcase Ventilation* valve. You will find this valve located in a rubber line that goes from the breather cap to a rubber grommet atop the valve cover. The valve is held in place by being pressed into the rubber grommet. Now PCV valves are either good or bad, with no in-between at all. To test yours, start the engine, then remove the hose and valve together from the rubber grommet. Place your finger over the end opening of the valve. If you feel the flow of air, there's nothing wrong with your PCV valve, and it can be put back in place. However, if it is static and you feel no air at all, buy a new valve for the year, make and model of your own car, remove the old valve by simply pulling it out of the hose, and then install the new unit. Test again for air pressure to make sure that you've done the job properly.

The Old Oil-Burner

After a car starts to age, you may suspect that it is "burning oil." The indications of this require a bit of detective snooping. If you notice that you must add oil between changes, yet see no signs of oil dripping under your car when it is allowed to sit overnight, you can suspect that oil is being burned. The car will also have a heavy smoking from the exhaust that is not simply condensate. If you constantly have to replace oil and see a puddle under the car,

you've got a leak that must be found and repaired.

When the car is burning oil, it means that crankcase oil is getting into the firing chambers of the cylinders.

As each piston moves up and down in the cylinder, a good seal is required between the piston and the cylinder. This is accomplished by the piston ring which girdles the piston and exerts an outward pressure against the wall. If oil is able to seep into the combustion chamber, it means that the ring is worn and needs replacement. This is called a "ring job," and requires the services of a mechanic.

However, there *is* a form of ring job that you can try yourself, on a maybe basis. If it works, it was worth the time and money, and if it doesn't you aren't a lot worse off than you were when you started.

There are several products available called "piston seal." These come in collapsible tubes, and to use it, you remove the spark plugs and squirt some of the gunk into each cylinder through the spark-plug hole. You then replace the plugs and start the engine, allowing it to reach operating temperature.

The black goo will line the walls of the cylinder, and hopefully create a seal that will stop the passage of oil into the combustion chamber.

If this fails, the mechanic will remove the head cover of the engine, take out the pistons, and replace them with oversize rings. He may bore the cylinders to a larger diameter if the inner surfaces have been gouged.

The Valves

Inside the engine block are the valves. There are nominally two valves per cylinder, an intake and an exhaust. After years of constant use, these valves and the valve seats can become pitted or corroded. Naturally, when this happens, they will not seat properly, and the valves and seats have to be re-ground. While you can, with diligence and patience, do this job yourself, it is one that is usually relegated to a skilled and well-equipped mechanic. However, if the build-up of carbon is only slight, what is involved is removing the valve

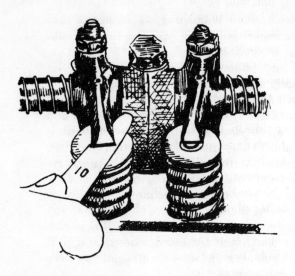

1 Make sure that the valve is fully closed, using the rule given below, by turning the engine over slowly by hand. Check the existing clearance gap with the correct size of feeler gauge.

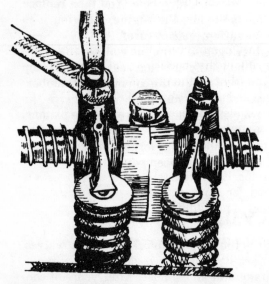

2 Loosen the lock-nut with a spanner and adjust the screw until the correct gap is obtained. Check with the feeler gauge. Hold the screw in position with the screwdriver, and tighten up the lock-nut with the wrench.

TO ENSURE VALVE IS FULLY CLOSED:
Follow the rule of 9 for a four cylinder engine (13 for a six cylinder). For example, turn the engine until valve 2 (counting from the front of the engine) is fully open, subtract 2 from 9 (or from 13 on a six cylinder) and valve 2 (or 11) will be fully closed.

springs using a special spring-compressing tool, and then lifting the valve out. The area is thoroughly cleaned, and then the valve is replaced in its seat, with a layer of "lapping compound" between the valve and seat. Using a drill motor and a special chuck, the valve is rotated on the seat until it is polished to a high brilliance and a good seal is effected. The area is again thoroughly cleaned, and the valve spring and valve are replaced.

The rocker-like devices that raise the valves in proper sequence are called the "tappets" and they can develop a characteristic noise of their own when in need of adjustment. Again, this is a matter of coordinating the lifting of the valves with the firing of the cylinders. While you can do it yourself, you can make matters worse, so you might be better off leaving this job to your mechanic.

A temporary cure for tappet noise is a good oil additive which is added directly to the crankcase. While this will not correct any problems, it will hide the tappet noise quite efficiently until you can have the work done.

Belts

The various rotating components under the hood may be driven by a belt and pulley arrangement, connected to the crankshaft of the engine. The belts are usually a rubberized fabric, and the pulleys are steel. Rest assured that the pulleys will last a lot longer than the belts will, and when a belt wears, it will have to be replaced. Removing a worn or damaged belt is the easiest thing in the world. In fact, in most cases, the old belt will let you know that it wants replacing, for it will simply fall off. You may not even find the old belt in the car when you are ready, new belt in hand, to effect the replacement.

Most of the belt system uses what are called "bogies," which are idler wheels whose only function is to take up slack. To mount a new belt, begin by loosening the bracket which holds the idler wheel, then put the belt in place over the driving pulley and the driven pulley. Place the bogie in position and then press it as hard as you can against the belt so that no slack is evident. Tighten the bogie bracket and the installation is complete.

While belts are designed to provide only a minimum amount of stretch, you may find that after installing a new belt, some slack has developed. In this case, simply loosen the bogie bracket, tighten the belt to remove the slack, and then re-tighten the bogie bracket.

Some belt-driven components might not have a bogie, but instead are themselves mounted in slotted mounting holes so the part itself can be shifted to take up belt slack.

Carburetor

The carburetor is relatively easy to dismount and clean, but keep in mind that it is a delicate mechanism. It is fairly easy to damage during the cleaning process.

It is accessible by removing the air breather assembly and then loosening the mounting bracket that holds the carburetor to the engine. Before you attempt this job, however, get a carburetor "kit" from your auto supply shop, and replace those parts offered in the kit that are subject to wear.

While the carburetor controls the balance of fuel to air, and also determines the amount of mixture that is vaporized, the settings for these controls is a delicate balance. Follow the manufacturer's recommendations for the procedures in setting these controls.

Because the carburetor does a delicate job in a rough atmosphere, its internal or throat parts can stick and bind. Cleaning these parts can only result in better performance, provided some care is taken.

Keep in mind that, after cleaning and before assembly, the parts should be kept on a dry, lint-free surface. If these delicate parts are allowed to pick up dirt or grit, you can wind up with a bigger mess than when you started. After cleaning and reassembling, re-mount the carburetor in proper alignment on the engine intake, replace the air breather and you should notice immediate improvement in engine operation.

Timing

In the old days, the timing was controlled by a lever at the steering column. You had to adjust the spark lever so the electricity went to the correct spark plug at the correct time. If you did not, you got what was called detonation, and backfiring. Many of the young gay blades used to attract attention to themselves by deliberately advancing the spark so that a sound like a gun shot would be heard when an attractive miss with a well-turned ankle was seen on the street. He made his car backfire and the girl would turn around in surprise. Our hero would tip his hat and smile. The girl would blush demurely, and such was the course of romance in those days.

Today, the timing is established and controlled automatically, and if your car backfires, you'd better plan on doing some work. The object, of course, is to have the spark plug ignite the fuel just before the piston reaches the apex of its stroke. It is the timing that achieves this, and determines at what point the piston will be driven downward again by the burning gases.

To adjust the timing, you need a device called a timing light. These can be had for well under twenty dollars. And it comes equipped with two wires. One is attached to the first spark plug, the other to ground. As you start the car's engine, you will see a bright, blue-white flash coming from the timing light with each firing of that particular spark plug.

At the front of the crankshaft, a line is inscribed, and as the shaft rotates, the line becomes visible with each firing of the light. The object is to adjust the position of this line by rotating the distributor cap while the line is being observed. The booklet that comes with the timing light will detail the exact position required for your car. This stroboscopic adjustment is not a difficult one to make, and because we are dealing with a mechanical device, setting the timing for one spark plug will correct the timing for all of them.

In-General Terms

Outside of what has been outlined here, there is little that you can do for your car's engine. However, for best performance, the engine should be kept as clean as possible. Periodic treatment with a steam jenny will help toward this end, as this will remove the build-up of impacted grease that has been baked into place.

Once you have cleaned the engine in this manner, an occasional wiping with a rag and some degreaser will keep the engine in topnotch clean condition.

Now you know some of the things that you can do to help maintain your engine in good operating condition and have learned which jobs require the services of a mechanic and should not be attempted by the do-it-yourselfer.

One of the biggest assets that you can obtain, should you want to work on your car's engine, is a mechanic's guide book for your own model car. Available in most bookstores, they detail disassembly procedures and offer many factory tips for the maintenance of your own automobile. They cost approximately ten to fifteen dollars each, and give you the same information that your mechanic uses when he works on your automobile. Be careful, however, that you use only the tools specified, for you can wreak havoc on your car's engine by using improper equipment.

In the next chapter, we are going to talk about a little-known area, that of glass and glazing.

10
Glass and Glazing

A scientist once explained that glass is not a solid—it's a liquid in the super-cooled state. Maybe so, but to all intents and purposes, it's solid as far as we're concerned. In the old days when cars first burst upon the scene, transparent mica was used for the windows, but this was soon replaced by glass and even the glass underwent some radical changes.

The first of these was what we now call "shatterproof" glass. This is a laminate consisting of two sheets of glass that are bonded to a sheet of plastic. This glass sandwich will not allow the glass to spall and shatter, thereby reducing the element of danger when an accident occurs.

Glass also took on some new shapes and curves, instead of the flat sheets that were used previously. This allowed the designers to introduce new curves and outlines to the cars.

In your window glass, you will also find that there are some fairly clever innovations. You may find a graduated tint applied near the top of your windshield which serves to reduce sun glare. Your front windshield might also have the car's radio antenna built in, in the form of a fine-wire dipolar element. And your rear window might have a heating element built in to reduce icing on the outside and fog on the inside.

When glass in your car is damaged, you will want to have it replaced. You might attempt to remove the old glass, and you could very well succeed. But when it comes to installing a new sheet of glass, you find yourself up against the first of several problems, namely, that the dealer will not sell the glass to you.

You see, people who buy automotive glass can be planning to do only one thing with it, and that's to install it. The auto glazier knows this, and also is aware that by selling you the glass, he does himself out of an installation fee. Oh, he will argue that special tools and knowledge are required, and he may be right. If you watch as he does his work, you will see that the channels must be properly cleaned, the new glass properly seated and the brackets and trim properly fastened. If you try to do this yourself and fail, you will develop all kinds of problems from leakage to undue stresses that can result in damage to your new pane or "light" as it is called.

However, there are certain types of problems that you can contend with and achieve some measure of success.

Basically, what you *have* to know about glass is that you must clean it. If you do not keep the glass clean, in time, it can discolor.

Small Holes

Obviously, we're not simply going to tell you that all you can do with the glass is clean it. There are other things that can go wrong, that you can really do something practical about.

If you've been following a gravel truck, or perhaps come across some exuberant youngster with an air rifle, you can get a pinhole puncture in the glass. What happens is that a high-speed projectile will impact on the outer surface of the glass and cause spalling on the inside. The result is a pinhole puncture in the glass, with a small hole at the outside and a larger, funnel-shaped hole on the inside. When such damages occur, you may be reluctant to replace the entire windshield, and if the damage is off to the side where it does not interfere with your visibility, you can live with it. But such pinholes in a driving rain can cause leakage, and the rough outer edges can play havoc with your wiper blades.

Get a tube of transparent silicone rubber. This stuff is used for tub caulking in the white, and the transparent product is best suited to the kind of repair we're going to talk about here.

Clean the glass thoroughly, then, using a toothpick, apply a small amount of the silicone to the hole, filling the hole completely. Do not attempt to level the inner spalled surface, but rather, simply close the hole to the outside. Allow the material to dry thoroughly, then use a sharp razor blade to trim the excess away.

You may feel that the relatively soft silicone product is less glasslike than some of the common household cements that are more rigid. Those acrylics do indeed dry to an almost glasslike consistency, but this is the very cause of the problems that they have! They will not expand at the same rate as glass, and will flake loose after the first climatic change. The more flexible silicones will give and flex as the glass expands and contracts, giving you a better, more long-lasting seal and maintaining the car's weatherproof integrity.

Leaking

One major problem with window glass in cars has nothing to do with the glass itself—it's leakage around the window seals. Such leakage can seep down through window channeling and into the car's trunk, and you'll be hard-pressed to locate the source of the leak, which you must do before you can effect a repair.

One of the best ways to accomplish this is with your garden hose. Play it over the suspect areas until you see water running through. To help in this work, we have found that you can apply a fine dusting of powder over the inside of the glass. One that is very effective is a foot powder in aerosol spray form. This will adhere to the window glass on the inside, dry to a fine white powder, and when a leak occurs, the rivulets of water quickly reveal the source of your problem. After a repair is effected, you can easily clean the powder from the glass.

Using a small kitchen spatula, raise the rubber grommet around the area of the leak, and inject as much of the silicone rubber inside the grommet as you can. Remove the window moulding, and apply an additional bead of silicone under that. In most cases, this will stop the leakage completely.

Watch the Accessories

The windshield wiper blades are meant to be replaced periodically. You might be interested to know that, in Russia, when a man parks his car, he removes the wiper blades and puts them either in his trunk or glove compartment. If he fails to do this, they will most certainly be stolen!

You know that your wiper blades need replacing when they smear the window instead of clearing it. We've seen some conditions where blades have so far gone that the metal arms contact the windshield. This can only cause abrasion and damage.

One of the things that causes much blade damage is ice and snow. On a cold day, you have the car's heater on and this heats the inside of the windshield. It begins to snow, and the first layers of snow, landing on the warm windshield, will melt. When the car cools sufficiently, this wet snow becomes ice and additional snow piles on top of that.

When you get back in the car, you brush the loose snow away from the windshield and find the wiper blades frozen fast to the glass. If you try to tear the blades loose, you're going to damage them. Neither should you turn the wipers on until the ice has been removed from the glass completely, as the hard, lumpy ice will unevenly wear the blades to a point where they must be replaced.

Hacking at the ice with an ice scraper isn't the answer either. This can mar and scratch the glass.

What should you do? Get in the car, start the engine, turn on the defrosters and wait until the windshield ice has softened to a point where it can easily be removed. Brush the ice away with an ice scraper and then turn on the wiper blades.

The wiper blades are *not* designed to remove ice—just water.

If you're impatient and can't wait for the car to heat up, you can obtain a device similar to a hair dryer that plugs into the cigarette lighter socket. With it, and the hot stream of air that it blows, you can completely melt the ice from your windshield.

Another problem that is easy to rectify is steam on the inside of the windows. Windshield steam can be removed by the car's defrosters. But steam that collects on the rear and side windows is another problem. However, you can obtain accessory defrosters that mount on the trunk shelf and blow steam from the rear window, or you can obtain transparent plastic sheets that attach easily to other windows and that keep steam and fog from forming. Electrical panels sealed in plastic are available, and these do a yeoman job as well.

If all else fails, you can try mixing a batch of liquid detergent and water, and apply this to the inside surfaces. While a temporary measure that will need repeating frequently, the detergent provides a wetting action that keeps the fog from forming into opaque globules.

When window glass repairs are needed, get them done. We've seen people driving with flapping sheets of plastic wrap over a missing window. These jury-rig solutions are dangerous at best.

One last word of caution. We've seen people trying to clear the insides of their car windows by wiping with a bare hand. If you do this, skin oils will be deposited on the inner surfaces of the glass and will be exceedingly difficult to remove. You'll be driving with smudging and reflected glare as a result. Instead, keep a clean cloth on the seat next to you. When you do get

fogging, wipe the windshield with this cloth.

We've run into some other problems with window glass. You're driving at night, and the reflection of your own dashboard on the windshield interferes with your vision. Before you frantically try to take corrective steps, determine what the cause of the trouble is. If it's the lighting of your dashboard, try turning down the intensity of the dashboard lights to reduce the reflection. If it is the dashboard or the trim, the answer might lie in a less-shiny dash treatment. You can accomplish this by painting the dash with dead flat black paint, or by applying a non-glare sheet of Contact paper.

Contact Paper

When you have to apply this stuff in large sheets, and don't know the little trick we're going to teach you now, it can be messy. The stuff sticks to itself, is hard to position, and sticks where you don't want it to.

Here comes the trick. Mix a sink full of detergent and warm water. Cut the correct length of paper that you need, then peel off the backing and put the sheet under the water. The water and detergent will wet the sticky surfaces so they won't stick to anything, not even themselves.

Now you can put the contact in place, slide it around to the position you need, and then just let the water dry. Now press it down, and it will adhere without a change in position. Use a razor blade to trim it to shape. Got an air bubble? Puncture it with a pin, and work the air out through the pinhole. When you have removed the air, the bubble will vanish, and you'll never see where the pinhole was.

One last tip.

Should you break one of the small round glass plates over a meter or gauge, you can replace it with another trick that you will simply have to try for yourself before you'll believe it.

Fill a basin with water, place a sheet of 1/16th-inch glass into the basin and, using an ordinary pair of household shears, you can cut the glass as if it were cardboard. The water equalizes the pressures and keeps the glass from cracking or chipping. You can simply mark the correct size circle, and cut it out to fit your dash panel!

11
Body Work

In a quite similar vein, similar to what we've told you thus far, there are certain things you are no doubt willing to do, and others that you shun like the plague.

Wash the car? Sure you will. It's no problem. You might, on an overly ambitious Sunday afternoon, even be willing to apply a coat of wax. But take out a dent? Apply a coat of paint? Not on your mudguard, you won't! Well, the washing and the waxing are beneficial to the car's body, and you most certainly should continue this process, or have it done for you by your children to earn a Sunday afternoon movie treat. Many areas of our country are subject to wearing factors in the atmosphere, and washing and waxing is the only way to remove these foul elements before they can damage the paint. But we want to go a few steps farther, and see if we can't spare you some of your own hard-earned money.

Bubble Dents

Sometimes, as the result of a light tap or smack by another car's fender, a deep, dished dent will appear in your own. If the dent is in a fender, or some other component where the reverse side is accessible, immediately reach under, ball your hand into a fist, and give the dent a mighty smack. You may be lucky enough to knock it back into its proper shape this way, but you have to move fast, before the metal sets.

Sometimes, the paint may be knocked loose, too, as a result of such ministrations, but even if this happens, it's a lot cheaper to have the area spray painted than to have it banged out by a body man. He'd have to paint it anyway, wouldn't he?

If such a dent occurs in an area where the rear of the surface is not accessible, such as in a door panel, get hold of one of those plumber's helpers plungers, wet the thing, and smack it right over the dent. Apply a mighty tug, and the dent might just pop out.

Deeper Dents

If you should get a dent that will not respond to the previous treatment, you have to resort to more forceful measures.

There's a tool called a slide hammer that consists of a weight which slides along a bar, to a stop. The bar is fitted with a strong hook-like device at the end away from the stop. You drill a small hole in the deepest part of the dent, hook the hammer through this hole, and operate the weighted slide against the stop to actually pull the metal back toward the surface. You may have to repeat this at several points in the dent to bring it back near the level.

The next step, of course, is to use a metal file to make sure that no raw metal protrudes beyond the exterior finish of the car. Satisfied that you have reached this point with no trouble, obtain a suitable fiberglass filler compound, and apply it liberally to the dent, filling all the areas. Use a straight-edge to strike or level the fiberglass so it follows the contours of the surface on which you are working. When the compound has dried, use a coarse rasp to remove whatever surface imperfections remain, and then sandpaper or emery cloth to provide as even a finish as you can.

On smaller surface dents, of course, the hammering can be eliminated, and you can simply re-surface dents with the fiberglass alone.

An Alternative

One very good standby, when a car's body component gets a dent or ding, is to simply replace the entire component.

If your car has its fenders attached by bolts, for example, it's a relatively simple matter to remove the damaged component, visit your local automobile junk yard, and purchase a replacement that is in good condition. Chances are that you won't be able to match the color, but don't let this throw you. We can always repaint later on.

This process holds good for fenders, doors, hood and trunk.

It's usually a two-man job to re-mount such components, for until such time as they are

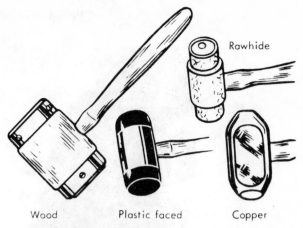

To remove dents without creating more damage than you are trying to cure, use a soft-faced mallet or non-ferrous hammer.

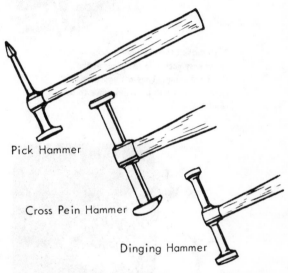

Special hammers for metalwork should be used only by the more experienced.

secured to the car's body, they may be subject to twisting or other strain which would damage the new part.

Back to the Surface

The film of paint on your car is a thin one, and, depending on how you've kept the car, and where you've kept it, chances are that when you do work on a car's body, you're going to want to paint the entire car to make sure that you get an even match of color.

Naturally, you're probably going to decide on a color, just for starters, and while there's no

1 Remove fittings where necessary to allow easy access to the back of the damaged panel. Take off any damaged parts, as they will probably have to be replaced

2 To beat out the dent use a soft-headed hammer or a tool especially designed for the job. Support the front of the area with the hand. Be careful not to beat it out too far.

3 Remove paint to bare metal with an electric drill and coarse sanding disc.

4 Mix just enough filler so that you don't end up with a lot of solidified, wasted paste, and apply it with a plastic or hardboard trowel in many thin layers.

When the filler is dry, use increasingly fine grades of wet and dry sandpaper to obtain a silky finish ready for priming and painting.

real harm in that, there are other matters that we have to concern ourselves with first.

Begin by carefully examining the car. Are there any dents or dings that might need fixing before we paint? If so, take care of those now, for you will not be able to fix them after painting.

Now inspect the chrome trim. If any of that needs replacing, obtain the replacements and then remove the old trim. We're going to paint the car first and *then* replace the trim.

Now we want to protect those parts that are not to be painted, and we do this with paper masking tape and some old newspaper. Place the newspaper over all the glass, and use a sharp razor blade to cut it to fit. Take pains not to cut into the rubber gasketing that holds the glass in place. Apply the masking tape so that all of the glass and rubber is covered, and the surface to be painted is fully exposed.

Make sure that you mask all trim, lamps, and moldings, as well as handles, and decorative surfaces. We've found that while you can mask the small trim with tape alone, using a razor blade, an old retoucher's trick works even better.

Your local art supply shop will yield a small bottle of a red, rubbery liquid called "frisket." Paint this liberally over a surface to be masked, and then go around the edges with a razor knife. The parts that are not to be masked are then peeled away. After painting, simply rub your finger over the frisket, and it will peel away, leaving the part under it clean and shiny.

Back when this writer had one of his first automobiles (it was a 1939 Ford, I think) there were special "powder-puff paints" which were paints with a high surface tension. You wiped them over the car's surface with a ladies powder puff, and they dried clean and shiny.

Today, your best shot is going to be to spray-paint the car, and you can rent a suitable compressor and spray gun. But begin with a good primer coat first, to cover any bare metal that may result from your earlier ministrations. The primer will form a good base for the finish coat, and will protect the car's metal under the paint. Allow the primer to dry thoroughly before applying the finish coat, and go over the primer with some fine sandpaper, too.

Now we're almost ready to begin. However, if you do not have a suitable dust-free garage to do your painting in, select a place where atmospheric dust will be held to a minimum, and where the direct rays of the sun will not be shining down to heat up the car's surface. In fact, a dull, grey day is best for painting the car.

Now wet down the area, using your garden hose to soak everything so that dust will not rise and settle on the new paint. Dust can ruin the finish.

Ready now? You've followed the manufacturer's instructions, mixed the paint and thinned it properly. Load up the gun, turn on the compressor, and let 'er go. Apply the paint in long, sweeping arcs, starting the pressure on the trigger before you reach contact with the surface and stopping the paint flow after you pass the surface. Remember that several thin coats are better than one heavy one, which is more likely to drip and run. Should a drip occur, wipe it away immediately and respray that area. When you've finished spraying the car, allow it to dry completely before removing the masking.

After the paint has dried, allow it to set for a couple of weeks before washing or waxing the surface. You will notice certain dried areas where the paint has dulled. These are called "orange peel" and you remove them by gently rubbing with a body compound, which is a light abrasive in cream form. Finish the job with a good rubbing wax, and your car will look almost like new.

Minor Scratches

All of the paint manufacturers sell "touch-up" paints to hide small surface scratches in the paint. But we've never been satisfied with the match of color or the ultimate results. In fact, some of the so-called touch-up jobs look far worse than the original scratch did.

We've found a much better way.

Get a box of assorted color crayons, sold at any 5¢ and 10¢ store or toy shop. Select the crayon that most closely matches the paint on your car, and then, on a nice warm day, rub the colored wax into the scratch by vigorously rubbing the crayon across the scratch. With your finger, press the wax hard into the gouge and let it set for awhile.

Now use a soft cloth (your old T-shirt is ideal) and rub in the direction of the scratch to remove the excess wax. Be gentle. When you have brought the wax to the surface of the paint, go over the whole thing with some good body wax, and then just *try* to find where the scratch was.

Vinyl Roofs

Got a vinyl roof on your car? Chances are that it is, at the very least, ready for some cleaning up.

Consult your telephone yellow pages to find a well-stocked auto supply store for a can of vinyl cleaner. Begin by washing the car's vinyl roof with any good detergent and water, and allow it to dry. Apply the liquid vinyl cleaner with a rag and, following the instructions on the container, buff it down. This will remove all the road grime and weathering, but you aren't finished yet. The next step is to apply a vinyl conditioner. This is available in a spray can, and consists of microscopic particles of vinyl in a suspension. You are really applying a new, clear surface coat of vinyl to the roof, and when this dries, it will look like a new vinyl top.

If you should get a tear in your vinyl roof, you can quickly and easily repair the tear with one of the many liquid-vinyl repair kits available. The principle is simple. Vinyl is a liquid that solidifies under heat.

Begin by preparing the tear. This is done by using a sharp razor blade to cut the sides of the rip clean and parallel, so that no threads of the backing material protrude. Cut the ends of the tear nice and round, so the rip can't proceed further.

Place a piece of cambric or linen backing cloth under the tear, so the mend will be properly reenforced. Now mix your colors to get as close a match as you can to the vinyl on your roof. Keep in mind that, unlike paint, liquid vinyl dries and sets in precisely the color that you mix. If neither darkens nor lightens.

From the assortment of graining papers furnished with the vinyl repair kit, select the one that most closely approximates the vinyl grain on the car. Clean the area to be repaired thoroughly, and then, using masking tape, attach one side of the graining paper, face down, so it covers the tear. Fold along the masking tape, using the tape as a hinge.

Spoon the mixed liquid vinyl into the tear, working some under the sides of the tear to form a good bond with the cloth underneath. Fold the graining paper over the tear and then, using a suitable heating tool (an ordinary electric iron heated to maximum will do), press the hot iron over the back of the graining paper for ten seconds. Remove the iron, and allow the patch to cool. Now you can lift the graining paper away. You will see that the repair is perfect, except for a characteristic dullness. Using a good vinyl finish, rub the chemical over the area you just repaired, and this will impart a luster that will match the rest of the car's roof. You will be hard-put to find where the rip was! In the same way you can make repairs to vinyls inside the car applying the same techniques.

As you may have gathered, preventive maintenance, in the form of periodic cleaning and waxing, will do much to enhance your automobile's appearance, and will keep it in like-new condition much longer.

12
The Last Word

All through this book, we have been telling you about things that you can purchase from your "local auto supply shop." While most of the urban areas do indeed have such shops around the nearest corner, the nearest corner in rural places could be ten miles away. However, we have done a bit of researching, and have learned that the automotive equipment manufactured for sale by some of the large department and catalog stores are produced under their own private brand label by the major parts manufacturers. We have also learned that you can often buy such equipment at a much-reduced price, thanks to the mass-buying economies that such large chains can take advantage of. What this means is that the shock absorbers that you buy from Sears Roebuck, for example, will have their own brand name. Yet these can be the same specification as a better-known brand, and save you a lot of money. Do not rule out purchases from such stores, especially when they run their special sales.

J. C. Whitney is a mail-order company that has everything that you will ever need for your car, whatever that car may be. If you're looking for a hard-to-find item, write to them. Once you're on their mailing list, you'll be getting a new catalog every few months, with hundreds of new items in it. If you're at all interested in automobiles, you'll be hard-pressed *not* to send them an order each time you get a new catalog.

While it will not sound like much of a good idea on the face of it, by all means visit your local automotive junk yard. You can often pick up an excellent bargain at these places, and benefit from another trick that we've used with great success.

These places usually offer equipment at two different prices. They charge one price if you want the component you've selected handed to you over the counter, and a much lower price if you will remove it from a wrecked car yourself, thus saving them the cost of the time to do it.

By taking off the part from a car just like yours yourself, you not only get the part at a lower price, you also gain the experience of removing it. We've never done this without learning a thing or two about how it's mounted or connected, making the installation job on our own car much easier.

Heating Things Up

There is a fanatical group of people who concern themselves with taking what they like to call "Detroit Iron" and doing things to it that are simply amazing. To get higher rates of compression, they shave the cylinder head. They remove the Detroit carburetor and replace it with a four-barrel throat. And, while I can remember as a youngster changing to lowslung rear ends for a racier look, today's hot-rodder raises the rear end so he can add bigger rubber. You see the modern rod with its tailend carried high over wide rubber tires that impart better traction.

You might pull up alongside one of these "rods" at a red light, and listen to the sound of the engine at idle. "My gosh!" you might say, "If *my* car sounded like that, I'd rush to the nearest mechanic!"

What you don't understand is that the rod is tuned up for operation at high speed, not at idle. And when he leaves you in the dust as the light changes, you can see the point to it all.

These people are willing experimenters, and the very things that they experiment with today might well be standard equipment on tomorrow's cars. Be tolerant of their seeming eccentricities. All inventors are slightly odd anyway.

We met one youngster out in the woods with his car. He had completely filled the back of the car with old newspapers, telephone books, and odds and ends. When he accomplished this seemingly pointless feat, he took a .38 calibre pistol out of the glove compartment, stepped back about twenty feet, and fired three rounds through the rear window, placing them at the right lower corner. I cautioned him that any one of these might cause the glass to craze, but he was lucky, and drilled three perfect bullet holes. He then emptied the car, removing the three slugs that were trapped by the paper, and drove off happily.

We found out from some other youngsters what that was all about later. When people asked what caused the holes, he simply said "bullets," and refused to talk about it any further. His friends drew their own conclusions (erroneous conclusions to be sure) and this guy was a big man for a long time after!

Decorating the car, whether with bullet holes or fancy striping, is a fad that the kids seem to enjoy. After all, a youngster has few

enough possessions of his own, and those that he does have, he will value and want to personalize. In my own youth, you hired an "artist" who could paint stripes along the body of your car. The rest of the decoration would lean toward chrome additions, or whatever the local auto supply shop had on special that week.

Today, you can get gigantic decals for the rear window that tell what kind of a car you started with. You can get full-color mylar printed murals for your side panels. You can obtain graduated optical effects, or flame decals that look as if the entire engine was blazing. Or you can get lacy striping decals that are a lot easier to apply and cost a lot less than the old painted ones.

Modifications

If you're planning to paint your car anyway, before you do so, you might want to consider adding a few modifications. If you drive through any of the large, suburban housing complexes, you will see homes that once started out looking pretty-much alike. However, in time, the various residents have added dormers, ells, wings, and a variety of other things that give their homes a distinct appearance and make them different from the rest.

We are quite the same way with our cars.

While you may buy a car that has precisely what you want, chances are that it won't be too long before you start thinking in terms of additions that may make it easier to locate in a crowded parking lot. These additions can be simple things, such as a small statuette in the rear window. One chap we know got one of the plastic ice scrapers, cut it out with a scroll saw in the shape of a hand, and attached it to his radio antenna. When he parks in a busy parking lot, he simply pulls the antenna to its full length and never has any trouble finding where he left his car. It stands there waving at him, its "hand" in the air!

You can purchase fiberglass molded components for your car that are already shaped and faired to blend in with the car's contours. You can add tail fins in any extreme, you can add air scoops for the hood, portholes, or fancy imitation opera windows or landau bars. These can be cemented to the surface of your car with special fiberglass cements and, with a bit of sanding, they become a part of the car's new profile. Usually, they come treated with a grey paint primer. After you have them in place, simply have the car painted and you'll never know that they were not custom-installed.

Naturally, they impart a custom look to the car, and are very easy to install, not horrendously costly, and add to the overall appearance in most cases.

There are other items you can add to enhance your car's appearance. You can buy an easy-to-install "Targa" band, for example, that goes over the car's top and provides one more piece of chrome.

Fender skirts are an ever-popular item, as are the add-on strips of chrome mylar that are held in place with adhesive-backing.

Naturally, these additions are a function of taste entirely. While you may or may not approve of them, happily, it's still a free choice that you are offered, and if you care for these things, they are there for the buying.

Lighting Accessories

Your car comes equipped with standard lighting fixtures that are built in, but you may feel the need for additional accessory lighting. Notable among the add-ons, are special chrome-yellow add-on lamps that mount on the skirt between hood and bumper. These are then wired in and are controlled by a switch inside the car. When you are driving through fog, these lamps will cut through the fog and provide better visibility than you could have without them.

Another interesting accessory is a plastic device that attaches to the center of the headlamps with a suction cup. As you drive, the wind causes the blades of this device to rotate, and the rubber blades keep your lamp lenses clear! It's a great addition, unless you live in an area where they are likely to be lifted off and stolen.

While we are on the subject of lighting, as you may know, your lamps are incandescent types, but there is a quartz-iodine lamp available which will last longer and provide about four times the light output. When you have to replace headlamps, these are well worth looking into.

Wireless Devices

In certain parts of the country, radar speed traps are commonplace, and for under ten dollars, you can obtain a small passive device that mounts inside the car and buzzes loudly when you are approaching such a trap. It is called passive because it emits no signal of its own, operating only when it receives the radar waves that the police use to measure your speed.

We've checked with several law enforcement officials about these things and they are, indeed, completely legal. However, most law officers are not as interested in handing out summonses as they are in reducing accidents. They don't mind your having the receivers, for they will cause you to slow down and become conscious of the fact that you are driving a car.

In other parts of the country, when you say "I've got a radio in my car," chances are that you are talking about a two-way citizens band transceiver. These CB units mount under the dash, and are a boon to road travel. If you get stuck on the road, you can call for assistance, tell your family you're going to be home late for dinner, and there is an organized group of youngsters who listen to the emergency channel on a 24-hour-a-day basis. Get into any sort of trouble on the road and they'll be right out to help.

Finally

There you have it. We've tried to give you as complete a discussion as we could, but an automobile is a highly complex instrument. So many things can be in need of your attention that we can only hope to have covered most of them. We regret if a matter of great and particular importance to you was not discussed because, in these pages, we have become friends with a common bond—a desire for better performance from our vehicles, and a way to shave some of the cost of maintaining them. And, for my part, it's been worthwhile.

Glossary

Air Filter: Ringlike filter formed of foam or fiber. Placed in breather cap, it removes grit from air passing to carburetor.

Alnico magnet: A man-made ceramic magnet.

Ammeter (or Amperemeter): A device that measures amperes or current.

Anode: The plus or positive terminal of a battery.

Anti-freeze: Used to keep the coolant from freezing in winter, overheating in summer.

Battery: Device consisting of two or more cells for producing electricity. The battery produces direct current by chemical action of lead and sulphuric acid.

Bogies: Idler wheels used only to take up slack.

Brake Drum: Steel rim against which the brake lining moves when the brake pedal is depressed.

Brake Lining: Expendable material that presses against the brake drum when the brake pedal is depressed. The resulting friction stops the wheel which, in turn, stops the car.

Brake Shoe: Support and actuator to which the brake lining is attached either by rivets or adhesives.

Brake-adjusting Tool: Tool used to adjust level of brakes and brake pedal to compensate for brake-lining wear.

Breather Cap: Device mounted atop carburetor, equipped with an air filter, to ensure that clean air is delivered to carburetor.

Bumper Jack: Jack operating on ratchet principle to raise car by lifting bumper.

Camber: The vertical angle of the wheel on the car.

Carburetor: Device mounted atop engine. It takes in fuel from fuel line, air from breather cap, and delivers a mixture of fuel and air for engine operation.

Cathode: The negative or minus terminal of a battery.

CD (Capacitive Discharge) Ignition: An electronic ignition system that provides a hotter spark and reduces component wear.

Cell: One unit of a battery.

Chocks: Blocking devices used to keep a car's wheels from rolling. Important safety measure!

Clutch: Pedal used in manual transmission systems that disengages the engine power from the drive wheel while the gears are being changed.

Compression Stroke: That point at which the piston has risen to apogee in the cylinder and at which spark plug firing should occur.

Coolant: Liquid used to keep the engine from overheating (usually water).

Crankshaft: Shaft that runs the length of the car engine, fitted with cams to raise and lower valves, protruding at the front to a series of pulleys which activate other accessories. The crankshaft is also connected to the lower ends of the piston rods which apply impetus to make the shaft rotate.

Cylinder: Tubular channel in which piston operates.

Cylinder Head: Upper part of engine block. Used to cover cylinders.

Diaphragm: That flexible part of a pump that causes the liquid to move. Usually rubber.

Differential: Placed in the center of the rear axle, this set of gears allows a wheel to rotate in one direction while other rotates in the opposite direction, thus permitting the car to turn with no friction to overcome.

Dingers (also "Dollys"): Tools used to reduce sheet metal dents. Used in body work.

Dipstick: Measuring device inserted deep into a car's component to check the level of liquid contained therein.

Distributor: An electrical device of the rotating type. The automatic switch that makes an electrical impulse go to correct spark plug at the correct time.

Electrolyte: The liquid in a wet-cell battery.

Engine Block: The steel block that forms the body of the engine.

File Card: Wire brush with very short "bristles," used for cleaning files.

Fuel Filter: Filtering device that removes sedimentary dirt from gasoline.

Fuel Pump: Mechanical device that applies fuel under pressure from the tank, through fuel lines, to the carburetor.

Gapping Tool: A tool consisting of assorted springs or leaves, each of a different thickness. It is used to determine the gap or the terminal distance between spark plugs' electrodes.

Gasket: Resilient material used between metal parts to form a seal.

Gasket Cement: Adhesive used to bond gasket material in place.

Grabber Screwdriver: A screwdriver with a metal device on the tip that holds a screw in place on the driver. Especially helpful when working with small screws or in an area with limited access.

Graphite: A dry, powdered lubricant.

Grease Fitting: Metal intake designed to take grease gun nozzle. It leads to the area in a joint where grease will be required.

Grease Gun: Device for inserting heavy grades of grease under pressure.

High Compression: The state of the fuel-air mixture when there is a good seal of piston to cylinder wall.

Hubcap: Cover used over tire's lug nuts to keep them free of dirt, as well as for decorative purposes.

Hydrometer: A device for testing specific gravity. One type is used for batteries, another for anti-freeze.

Jack: Used to raise car and wheels off the ground to facilitate work.

Jumper Cables: Long, insulated wires used to connect another car's battery to your own system, enabling you to start your own car if the battery is weak.

Light: A pane of glass.

Low Compression: This state means that the fuel-air mixture in the cylinder is escaping past the piston, reducing overall efficiency.

Lug Wrench: Tool for removing the lugs or nuts from the wheels.

Master Cylinder: Part of the hydraulic system that activates the brake mechanism.

Oil Filler Cap: The cap or cover for the oil filler hole at the top of the valve cover.

PCV (Positive Crankcase Ventilation) Valve: The valve that connects from the breather cap to the crankcase to ensure proper airflow to crankcase.

Phillips-head Screw: A screw or bolt equipped with a "criss-cross" slot.

Piston: Metal disc that moves up and down in the cylinder as cam shaft rotates and cylinder firing occurs.

Piston Ring: Expandable sealing ring that keeps oil from entering the upper cylinder chamber and makes cylinder firing more efficient.

Pliers: Tool used for grasping and holding.

Points: Timing system used in distributor to determine that the spark is generated at crucial point of firing.

Radiator: The system of piping through which coolant flows. It is located at the front of the car, directly ahead of the fan.

Ratchet: A device which operates when rotated in one direction, and slips when rotated in the opposite direction.

Reamer: A steel-cutting device used to enlarge holes.

Regroove: An old tire which has been processed to deepen the grooves. No additional rubber is added.

Resistor Plug: A special spark plug with built-in resistor to suppress static noise.

Retread: An old used tire which has been processed to add additional rubber to the tread area.

Roll-on Ramps: A very secure system for raising one end of the car so that it can be worked on safely.

Screw Jack: A jack that operates on the threaded screw principle, as opposed to a bumper jack.

Shatterproof Glass: Glass formed in two sheets with a flexible plastic bonding between them to keep the glass from shattering or spalling.

Shock Absorbers (or Shocks): Devices attached between the car's frame and the axles to keep the vehicle from "motor-boating" or bouncing.

Silica Gel: A chemical desiccator which removes moisture and keeps tools and parts dry.

Sled: A wheeled board, often equipped with a padded headrest. The device is used by mechanics for comfort and convenience when working under a car.

Slide Hammer: A tool for pulling deep dents out of a car body.

Spark Plug: The electrical ignition device which ignites the fuel-air mixture in the cylinder.

Spark-Plug Wrench: A special tool designed for removing and re-installing spark plugs correctly and without damage.

Steam Jenny: A machine which generates live steam under high pressure. It is used for cleaning greasy engine blocks.

Tailpipe: Pipe running from muffler to exhaust point.

Thermostat: A valve operated by temperature. When the temperature is sufficiently high, the thermostat opens allowing coolant to flow.

Timing Light: A bright electronic lamp mounted in a special holder that connects to the spark plug. This device is used to make sure that the spark occurs at the peak efficiency point of the compression stroke.

Tire Bead: The raised portion of rubber around the edge of the tire. It serves to hold the inflated tire tight to the rim.

Tire Pressure Gauge: A device that determines the amount of air pressure in the tire.

Toe-in: The horizontal angle of the wheel on the car.

Torque Wrench: A wrench which has a dial that indicates the amount of applied torque, so that components are not over-tightened.

Transmission: The gears that are changed automatically (or by shifting) to provide maximum usable power between the engine and the drive wheels.

Valve Cover: Formed steel cover to protect the valves at the top of the engine. The valve cover keeps dirt and grit out, and lubricants in.

Valve Lifters (or Tappets): Mechanical devices used to regulate the intake and outlet valves in the cylinder head.

Valve Seat: Finely-honed surface against which the valve rests.

Web Wrench: A wrench formed of webbed belting and a rigid handle.

White Grease: An emulsion of water and grease.

Index

Page numbers in boldface type indicate illustrations